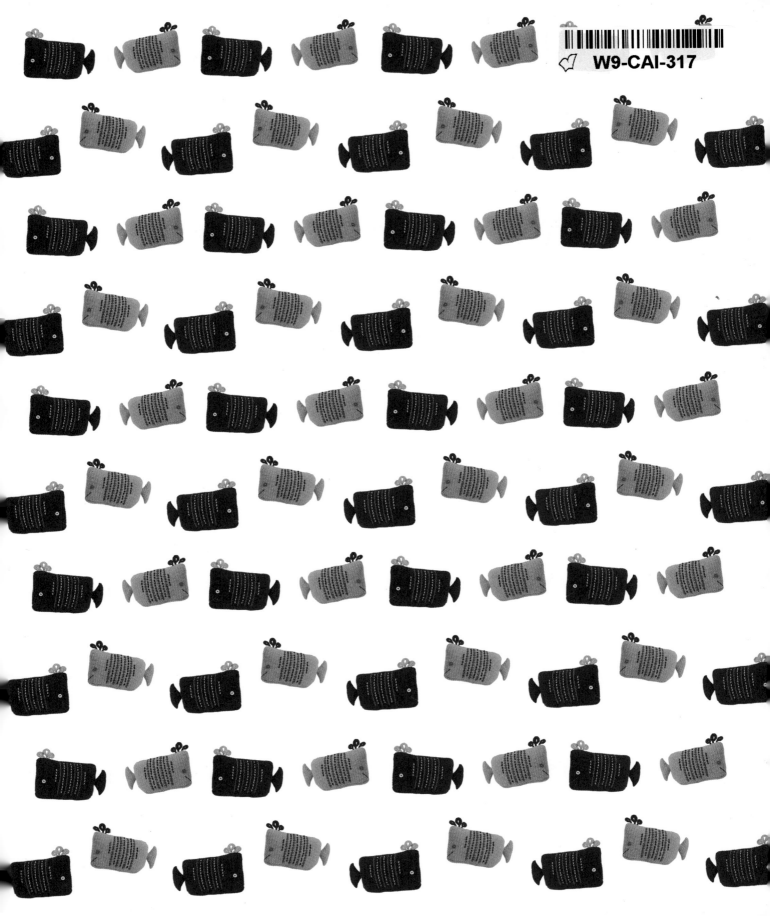

LUCINDA GUY

CROCHET DESIGNS FOR KIDS

20 PROJECTS TO MAKE FOR GIRLS & BOYS

LUCINDA GUY
CROCHET DESIGNS FOR KIDS
20 PROJECTS TO MAKE FOR GIRLS & BOYS

Illustrations by François Hall

TRAFALGAR SQUARE
North Pomfret, Vermont

First published in the United States of America by
Trafalgar Square Books
North Pomfret, Vermont 05053

Copyright © Rowan Yarns 2008
Text and design copyright © Lucinda Guy 2008

Designs by Lucinda Guy
Photography, illustrations, and layout by François Hall
Editor Sally Harding
Technical consultant/pattern writer Penny Hill
Pattern checker Tricia Mckenzie

Library of Congress Control Number: 2007908665

ISBN-13: 978-1-57076-387-8

10 9 8 7 6 5 4 3 2 1

Printed in China

CONTENTS

INTRODUCTION

The projects in this book are designed to inspire you to make wonderful and original items in very simple crochet for small kids to wear, use, and play with.

All the projects are suitable for both the beginner and more experienced crocheter alike, because only single or double crochet or easy-to-learn fancier stitches are used. While some of the garments can be made really quickly—such as the Summer Cap, Winter Warmers, and the Posy Headscarf—other projects, although essentially simple to crochet, will take a little longer and need just that extra bit of patience to assemble, such as the Bon-Bon Blanket or the Ariadne Doll.

If you are concerned that even these projects are not simple enough, remember that you can simplify them yourself. For example, you do not have to make the motifs for the garments—Milo for the Milo Owl Sweater, Marcel the Snail for the striped top, Bessie Bird for the coat, or the posies for the Posy Pinafore. You could also omit any stripes or embroidery and just make a plain garment. Obviously, I think that this would be a shame since these are the elements that bring the garments alive and make them stand apart from the ordinary.

So simplify if you must and change the colors to suit you, but above all, do be inspired and try some crochet!

SPRING

Soft, sweet, and gentle for spring, all these easily made designs are crocheted in a classic pure wool yarn that is machine washable.

Posy Pinafore (page 10)

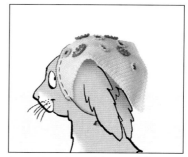

Posy Headscarf (page 16)

Marcel the Snail Top (page 20)

Little Stripy Bag (page 24)

Bon-Bon blanket (page 26)

SUMMER

Light, airy, and ideal for summer dressing, these simple projects are made in a fine cotton yarn that is also machine washable. Perfect!

Sweet Cicely Skirt (page 30)

Sweet Cicely Top (page 34)

Summer Cap (page 38)

Wilbur Whale (page 42)

Best Beach Bag (page 48)

FALL

Pure wool yarns are used for these easy and wonderful fall designs. Machine washable, they are not only stylish but also practical.

Dolores Dress (page 52)

Dolores Slippers (page 58)

Ariadne Doll (page 62)

Annie V-Neck Vest (page 68)

Cozy Connie Sweater (page 72)

WINTER

Cozy, warm pure wool is used to make these comforting winter items. Easy to make, easy to use, and wear, easily machine washable.

Bessie Bird Coat (page 76)

Milo Owl Sweater (page 86)

Winter Warmers (page 92)

Henri Elephant (page 96)

Zigzag Throw (page 104)

9

POSY PINAFORE

Sweet and lovely, this little pinafore is a must-have for spring. Keep it plain and simple with just a belt and buckle, or decorate the pockets with little flowers and pearly buttons. Then wear it with the headscarf on page 17 and the bag on page 25.

Then wear it with the headscarf on page 17 and the bag on page 25.

SIZES AND MEASUREMENTS

To fit ages (in years)	2–3	3–4	4–5
To fit chest	22in	24in	26in
	56cm	61cm	66cm
Finished measurements			
Around chest	26¾in	29in	31in
	68cm	74cm	79cm
Length to shoulder	19¾in	22in	25¼in
	50cm	56cm	64cm

YARN

Rowan *4-Ply Soft* (1¾oz/50g balls) as follows:

A	pink (Fairy 395)	3 balls	4 balls	4 balls
B	red (Honk 374)	2 balls	2 balls	2 balls
C	sage green (Leafy 367)	1 ball	1 ball	1 ball
D	pale blue (Whisper 370)	1 ball	1 ball	1 ball

HOOK

Size C-2 (2.5mm) crochet hook

EXTRAS

2 mother-of-pearl buttons ¾in/2cm in diameter, to fasten straps on pinafore
6 small buttons for flower centers (optional)
1 buckle

GAUGE

25 sts and 26 rows to 4in/10cm measured over sc using size C-2 (2.5mm) crochet hook *or size necessary to obtain correct gauge.*

ABBREVIATIONS

sc2tog = [insert hook in next st, yo and draw a loop through] twice, yo and draw through all 3 loops on hook—*one st decreased.*
See also page 110.

PINAFORE

FRONT

Using size C-2 (2.5mm) hook and B, ch 109 (121: 133).
Fasten off.
Change to A on next row as follows:
Foundation row (RS) Join A with a sl st to first ch, ch 1 (does NOT count as a st), 1 sc in same place as sl st, 1 sc in each of rem ch, turn. *109 (121: 133) sc.*
Row 1 (patt row) Ch 1 (does NOT count as a st), 1 sc in each sc to end, turn.
(Last row forms simple sc patt when repeated.)
Cont in sc throughout, work 2 rows more.
Next row (dec row) (RS) Ch 1, 1 sc in each of first 6 sc, work sc2tog over next 2 sc, 1 sc in each sc to last 8 sc, work sc2tog over next 2 sc, 1 sc in each of last 6 sc, turn.
Work even for 3 rows, ending with a WS row.
Rep last 4 rows 13 (15:17) times more and then the dec row again. *79 (87: 95) sc.*
Work even until Front measures 9¾ (11¾: 13¾)in/ 25 (30: 35)cm from beg, ending with a RS row.
Next row (WS) Ch 1, 1 sc in each of first 2 sc, [1 sc in each of next 6 sc, work sc2tog over next 2 sc] 9 (10: 11) times, work sc2tog over next 2 sc, 1 sc in each of last 3 sc, turn. *69 (76: 83) sc.***
Cut off A and change to B.
Work even for 10 rows, ending with a WS row.
Next row (RS) 1 sl st in each of first 8 (9: 10) sc, ch 1, 1 sc in same place as sl st, 1 sc in each sc to last 7 (8: 9) sc, turn. *55 (60: 65) sc.*
Next row (dec row) Ch 1, 1 sc in first sc, work sc2tog over next 2 sc, 1 sc in each sc to last 3 sc, work sc2tog over next 2 sc, 1 sc in last sc, turn.
Work even for 3 rows, ending with a RS row.
Rep last 4 rows 3 times more and then the dec row again. *45 (50: 55) sc.*
Work even until Front measures 17 (19: 21)in/

43 (48: 53) cm from beg, ending with a WS row.

Divide for straps
Next row (RS) Ch 1, 1 sc in each of first 9 (11: 13) sc, turn. 9 (11: 13) sc.
Working on these sts only for first strap, cont as follows:
Work even until strap measures 12½ (13½: 15¾) in/32 (34: 40) cm.
Fasten off.
With RS facing, return to sts left unworked, skip center 27 (28: 29) sc and rejoin B with a sl st to next sc, ch 1, 1 sc in same place as sl st, 1 sc in each sc to end, turn. 9 (11: 13) sc.
Work even until strap measures 12½ (13½: 15¾) in/32 (34: 40) cm.
Fasten off.

BACK
Work as given for Front to **
Cut off A and change to B.
Work even for 4 rows, ending with a WS row.
Work buttonholes over next 2 rows as follows:
Buttonhole row 1 (RS) Ch 1, 1 sc in each of first 19 (21: 23) sc, ch 4, skip next 4 sc, 1 sc in each sc to last 23 (25: 27) sc, ch 4, skip next 4 sc, 1 sc in each sc to end, turn.
Buttonhole row 2 Ch 1, *1 sc in each sc to 4-ch sp, 4 sc in 4-ch sp; rep from * once, 1 sc in each sc to end, turn.
Work even for 4 rows.
Fasten off.

POCKETS (make 2)
Using size C-2 (2.5mm) hook and B, ch 19.
Foundation row (RS) 1 sc in 2nd ch from hook, 1 sc in each of rem ch, turn. 18 sc.
Row 1 (patt row) Ch 1 (does NOT count as a st), 1 sc in each sc to end, turn.
(Last row forms simple sc patt when repeated.)
Cont in sc throughout, work 17 rows more, ending with a RS row.
Next row (WS) Ch 3 (to count as first dc), skip first sc, 1 dc in each sc to end. 18 sts.
Fasten off.

Picot pocket trimming
With RS of pocket facing and using size C-2 (2.5mm) hook and A, working trimming at top of pocket along last sc row as follows:
Row 1 (RS) Insert hook from front to back and through to front again around first 2 sc of last row of sc, yo and draw a loop through fabric and loop on hook, ch 4, 1 sl st in 4th ch from hook, *insert hook from front to back and to front again around next 2 sc, yo and draw a loop through fabric and loop on hook, ch 4, 1 sl st in 4th ch from hook; rep from * 7 times more.
Fasten off.

TO FINISH
Press pinafore pieces lightly on wrong side, following instructions on yarn label.
Sew side seams on pinafore.
Sew one button to end of each strap.
Using a blunt-ended yarn needle and A, work two large cross-stitches at center of pocket two rows apart as shown, working each one over 2 sc and two rows.
Sew pockets to front of pinafore as shown.

BELT

TO MAKE BELT
The belt (see page 14) is made in two halves, that are joined together lengthwise along the center.

First half
Using size C-2 (2.5mm) hook and D, ch 175 (182: 189).
Fasten off, leaving a long tail-end of yarn.
Foundation row (RS) Using B, join yarn with a sl st to first ch, ch 1 (does NOT count as a st), 1 sc in same place as sl st, 1 sc in each of rem ch, turn. 175 (182: 189) sc.
Fasten off.
Row 1 Using A, join yarn with a sl st to first sc, ch 1 (does NOT count as a st), 1 sc in same place as sl st, 1 sc in each sc to end.
Fasten off.

Second half
Work second half in same way as first half, but turn work at end of row 1 and do not fasten off A.
Place first half behind second half with right

sides of strips together and tops of last rows aligned, then still using A, join strips by working a row of sc through both pieces at once.
Fasten off.

Edging at ends
Using long tail-end of D, work a row of sc along each short end.
Fasten off.

BELT LOOPS (make 3)
Using size C-2 (2.5mm) hook and A, ch 8.
Foundation row (RS) 1 sc in 2nd ch from hook, 1 sc in each of rem ch, turn. 7 sc.
Row 1 Ch 1 (does NOT count as a st), 1 sc in each sc to end.
Fasten off.

TO FINISH
Press pieces lightly on wrong side, following instructions on yarn label.
Sew buckle to one end of belt.
Sew one belt loop to each side seam and one to the center of the back. Thread belt through loops.

FLOWER MOTIFS

LARGE FLOWERS (make 2)
Using size C-2 (2.5mm) hook and C, ch 4 and join with a sl st to first ch to form a ring.
Round 1 (RS) Using C, ch 1, 8 sc in ring, change to D and join with a sl st to first sc.
(Do not turn at end of rounds, but work with RS always facing.)
Round 2 Using D, ch 1, 2 sc in same place as sl st, [2 sc in next sc] 7 times, change to C and join with a sl st to first sc. *16 sc.*
Cut off D and cont with C.
Round 3 Ch 1, 2 sc in same place as sl st, 1 sc in next sc, [2 sc in next sc, 1 sc in next sc] 7 times, join with a sl st to first sc. *24 sc.*
Round 4 Ch 4, 1 sl st in 3rd ch from hook, 1 sl st in each of first 2 sc, [ch 4, 1 sl st in 3rd ch from hook, 1 sl st in each of next 2 sc] 11 times, join with a sl st to first of 4-ch. *12 picot petals.*
Work a 3in/7.5cm length of chain and fasten off.

SMALL FLOWERS (make 4)
Using size C-2 (2.5mm) hook and B, ch 4 and join

with a sl st to first ch to form a ring.
Round 1 Using B, ch 1, 9 sc in ring, change to D and join with a sl st to first sc.
(Do not turn at end of round, but cont with RS facing.)
Cut off B and cont with D.
Round 2 Using D, ch 4, 1 sl st in 3rd ch from hook, 1 sl st in first sc, [ch 4, 1 sl st in 3rd ch from hook, 1 sl st in next sc] 8 times, join with a sl st to first of 4-ch. *9 picot petals.*
Work a 3in/7.5cm length of chain and fasten off.

TO FINISH
Do not press flowers.
Sew one large flower and two small flowers to Front above each pocket as shown, securing ends of flower stems inside pockets.
If desired, sew a button to center of each flower.

POSY HEADSCARF

Perfect for those first days of spring and really simple to make, the Posy Headscarf is guaranteed to keep showers away and to make the sun shine—everyone must have one!

SIZES AND MEASUREMENTS

To fit ages (in years)	2–3	3–4	4–5
Finished measurement			
Width at widest	12in	12½ in	13in
	30cm	32cm	33cm

YARN

Rowan *4-Ply Soft* (1¾ oz/50g balls) as follows:

A	pink (Fairy 395)	1 ball	1 ball	1 ball
B	red (Honk 374)	1 ball	1 ball	1 ball
C	sage green (Leafy 367)	1 ball	1 ball	1 ball
D	pale blue (Whisper 370)	1 ball	1 ball	1 ball

HOOK

Size C-2 (2.5mm) crochet hook

GAUGE

25 sts and 26 rows to 4in/10cm measured over sc using size C-2 (2.5mm) crochet hook *or size necessary to obtain correct gauge.*

ABBREVIATIONS

sc2tog = [insert hook in next st, yo and draw a loop through] twice, yo and draw through all 3 loops on hook—*one st decreased.*

sc3tog = [insert hook in next st, yo and draw a loop through] 3 times, yo and draw through all 4 loops on hook—*2 sts decreased.*

See also page 110.

TO MAKE HEADSCARF

Using size C-2 (2.5mm) hook and B, ch 75 (79: 83).
Fasten off.
Change to A on next row as follows:
Foundation row (RS) Join A with a sl st to first

ch, ch 1 (does NOT count as a st), 1 sc in same place as sl st, 1 sc in each of rem ch, turn. *75 (79: 83) sc.*
Row 1 (patt row) Ch 1 (does NOT count as a st), 1 sc in each sc to end, turn.
(Last row forms simple sc patt when repeated.)
Row 2 (eyelet row) Ch 4 (to count as first dc and first 1-ch sp), skip first 2 sc, 1 dc in next sc, *ch 1, skip 1 sc, 1 dc in next sc; rep from * to end.
Row 3 Ch 1, 1 sc in first dc, *1 sc in next 1-ch sp, 1 sc in next dc; rep from * to last 1-ch sp, 1 sc in next 1-ch sp, 1 sc in 3rd of 4-ch, turn. *75 (79: 83) sc.*
Cont in sc throughout, work 2 rows.
Next row (dec row) (RS) Ch 1, 1 sc in first sc, work sc2tog over next 2 sc, 1 sc in each sc to last 3 sc, work sc2tog over next 2 sc, 1 sc in last sc, turn.
Work even for 1 row.
Rep last 2 rows until 5 sc rem, ending with a WS row.
Next row (RS) Ch 1, 1 sc in first sc, work sc3tog over next 3 sc, 1 sc in last sc, turn. *3 sc.*
Work even for 1 row.
Next row Ch 1, work sc3tog over 3 sc. *1 sc.*
Fasten off.

LARGE FLOWERS (make 4)

Using size C-2 (2.5mm) hook and C, ch 4 and join with a sl st to first ch to form a ring.
Round 1 (RS) Using C, ch 1, 8 sc in ring, change to D and join with a sl st to first sc.
(Do not turn at end of rounds, but work with RS always facing.)
Round 2 Using D, ch 1, 2 sc same place as sl st, [2 sc in next sc] 7 times, change to C and join with a sl st to first sc. *16 sc.*
Cut off D and cont with C.
Round 3 Ch 1, 2 sc in same place as sl st, 1 sc in next sc, [2 sc in next sc, 1 sc in next sc] 7 times, join with a sl st to first sc. *24 sc.*
Round 4 Ch 4, 1 sl st in 3rd ch from hook, 1 sl st in each of first 2 sc, [ch 4, 1 sl st in 3rd ch from hook, 1 sl st in each of next 2 sc] 11 times, join

with a sl st to first of 4-ch. *12 picot petals.*
Fasten off.

SMALL FLOWERS (make 6)
Using size C-2 (2.5mm) hook and B, ch 4 and join
with a sl st to first ch to form a ring.
Round 1 Using B, ch 1, 9 sc in ring, change to D
and join with a sl st to first sc.
(Do not turn at end of round, but cont with RS
facing.)
Cut off B and cont with D.
Round 2 Ch 4, 1 sl st in 3rd ch from hook, 1 sl st
in first sc, [ch 4, 1 sl st in 3rd ch from hook, 1 sl st
in next sc] 8 times, join with a sl st to first of 4-ch.
9 picot petals.
Fasten off.

TIE
Make a twisted cord for tie as follows:
Cut two strands of B, each approximately 2¾yd/
2.5m long. Align the strands and knot them
together at each end. Hook one end over a
door handle, and insert a pencil through the
other end. Twist pencil clockwise until strands
are tightly twisted. Holding cord in center with
one hand, bring ends together and let two
halves twist together.
Knot each end to make a finished cord 31in/
79cm long. Trim ends ¼in/1cm from knots.

TO FINISH
Do not press flowers.
Press headscarf lightly on wrong side, following
instructions on yarn label.
Sew flowers to right side of headscarf in
random positions.
Thread tie through eyelet row.

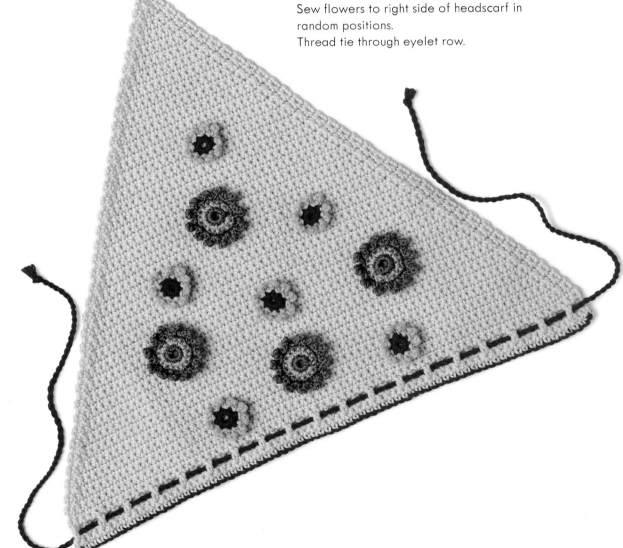

MARCEL THE SNAIL TOP

Snails are always out and about in the spring, and Marcel is no exception. Simple stripes and running-stitch detail make this little top extra special. Because it is so easily made in single crochet, you can be outside wearing it with the snails in no time!

TOP

BACK
Using size C-2 (2.5mm) hook and C, ch 85 (92: 99).
Fasten off.
Change to A on next row as follows:
Foundation row (RS) Join A with a sl st to first ch, ch 1 (does NOT count as a st), 1 sc in same place as sl st, 1 sc in each of rem ch, turn. *85 (92: 99) sc.*
Row 1 (patt row) Ch 1 (does NOT count as a st), 1 sc in each sc to end, turn.
(Last row forms simple sc patt when repeated.)
Cont in sc throughout, work in stripe sequence of [2 rows B, 2 rows A] repeated until Back measures 5¼ (5½: 6) in/13 (14: 15) cm from beg, ending with a WS row.
Cut off B.
Cont in A only, work until Back measures 6¼ (6¾: 7) in/16 (17: 18) cm from beg, ending with a WS row.

Shape armholes
Next row (RS) 1 sl st in each of first 8 (9: 10) sc, ch 1, 1 sc in same place as last sl st, 1 sc in each sc to last 7 (8: 9) sc, turn. *71 (76: 81) sc.*
Next row Ch 1, 1 sc in first sc, work sc2tog over next 2 sc, 1 sc in each sc to last 3 sc, work sc2tog over next 2 sc, 1 sc in last sc, turn.
Rep last row 4 times more. *61 (66: 71) sc.***
Work even until Back measures 10¼ (11: 11¾) in/ 26 (28: 30) cm from beg, ending with a WS row.

Shape back neck
Next row (RS) Ch 1, 1 sc in each of first 12 (13: 14) sc, work sc2tog over next 2 sc, 1 sc in next sc, turn. *14 (15: 16) sc.*
Working on these sts only for first side of neck, cont as follows:
Next row Ch 1, 1 sc in first sc, work sc2tog over next 2 sc, 1 sc in each sc to end, turn. *13 (14: 15) sc.*

SIZES AND MEASUREMENTS

To fit ages (in years)	2–3	3–4	4–5
To fit chest	22in	24in	26in
	56cm	61cm	66cm
Finished measurements			
Around chest	26¾in	29in	31in
	68cm	74cm	79cm
Length to shoulder	11in	11¾in	12½in
	28cm	30cm	32cm

YARN

Rowan *4-Ply Soft* (1¾oz/50g balls) as follows:

		2–3	3–4	4–5
A	charcoal (Sooty 372)	2 balls	2 balls	3 balls
B	pale blue (Whisper 370)	1 ball	2 balls	2 balls
C	sage green (Leafy 367)	1 ball	1 ball	1 ball
D	ecru (Linseed 393)	1 ball	1 ball	1 ball

HOOK
Size C-2 (2.5mm) crochet hook

EXTRAS
2 red buttons ⁷⁄₁₆in/11mm in diameter, for snail motif (snail is optional)

GAUGE
25 sts and 26 rows to 4in/10cm measured over sc using size C-2 (2.5mm) crochet hook *or size necessary to obtain correct gauge.*

ABBREVIATIONS
sc2tog = [insert hook in next st, yo and draw a loop through] twice, yo and draw through all 3 loops on hook—*one st decreased.*
See also page 110.

Next row Ch 1, 1 sc in each sc to last 3 sc, work sc2tog over next 2 sc, 1 sc in last sc, turn. *12 (13: 14) sc.*

Dec 1 st at neck edge on each of next 3 rows, working decreases as set. *9 (10: 11) sc.*

Fasten off.

With RS facing, return to sts left unworked, skip center 31 (34: 37) sc and rejoin A with a sl st to next sc, ch 1, 1 sc in same place as sl st, work sc2tog over next 2 sc, 1 sc in each sc to end, turn. *14 (15: 16) sc.*

Next row Ch 1, 1 sc in each sc to last 3 sc, work sc2tog over next 2 sc, 1 sc in last sc, turn. *13 (14: 15) sc.*

Next row Ch 1, 1 sc in first sc, work sc2tog over next 2 sc, 1 sc in each sc to end, turn. *12 (13: 14) sc.*

Dec 1 st at neck edge on each of next 3 rows, working decreases as set. *9 (10: 11) sc.*

Fasten off.

FRONT

Work as for Back to **.

Work even until 20 rows less have been worked than Back to fasten-off at shoulder, ending with a WS row.

Shape front neck

Next row RS) Ch 1, 1 sc in each of first 16 (17: 18) sc, work sc2tog over next 2 sc, 1 sc in next sc, turn. *18 (19: 20) sc.*

Working on these sts only for first side of neck, cont as follows:

Next row Ch 1, 1 sc in each sc to end, turn.

Next row Ch 1, 1 sc in each sc to last 3 sc, work sc2tog over next 2 sc, 1 sc in last sc, turn.

Rep last 2 rows until 9 (10: 11) sc rem.

Work even for 1 row.

Fasten off.

With RS facing, return to sts left unworked, skip center 23 (26: 29) sc and rejoin A with a sl st to next sc, ch 1, 1 sc in same place as sl st, work sc2tog over next 2 sc, 1 sc in each to end, turn.

Next row Ch 1, 1 sc in each sc to end, turn.

Next row Ch 1, 1 sc in first sc, work sc2tog over next 2 sc, 1 sc in each sc to end, turn.

Rep last 2 rows until 9 (10: 11) sc rem.

Work even for 1 row.

Fasten off.

TO FINISH

Press pieces lightly on wrong side, following instructions on yarn label.

Sew shoulder seams.

Neck edging

With RS facing and using size C-2 (2.5mm) hook and B, work edging along neck as follows:

Round 1 (RS) Join B with a sl st to neck edge at left shoulder seam, ch 1, 1 sc in same place as sl st, then work a round of sc evenly around neck edge, join with a sl st to first sc.

Fasten off.

With RS facing, join in D on next round as follows:

Round 2 (RS) Join D with a sl st to first sc at beg of last round, ch 1, 1 sc in same place as sl st, 1 sc in each sc to end of round, join with a sl st to first sc.

Fasten off.

With RS facing, join in C on next round as follows:

Round 3 (RS) Join C with a sl st to first sc at beg of last round, ch 1, 1 sc in same place as sl st,

1 sc in each sc to 1 sc before first of 2 corners on center front neck, work sc2tog over next 2 sc (to shape corner), 1 sc in each sc to 1 sc before second corner, work sc2tog over next 2 sc, 1 sc in each sc to end of round, join with a sl st to first sc.

Fasten off.

Armhole edgings (both alike)

Sew side seams.

With RS facing and using size C-2 (2.5mm) hook and B, work edging around each armhole edge as follows:

Round 1 (RS) Join B with a sl st to armhole edge at side seam, ch 1, 1 sc in same place as sl st, then work a round of sc evenly around armhole edge, join with a sl st to first sc.

Fasten off.

With RS facing, join in D on next round as follows:

Round 2 (RS) Join D with a sl st to first sc at beg of last round, ch 1, 1 sc in same place as sl st, 1 sc in each sc to end of round, join with a sl st to first sc.

Fasten off.

With RS facing, join in C and work next round as for round 2. Fasten off.

Embroidery

Using a blunt-ended yarn needle, work embroidery on top as follows:

Using C, work running stitches all around the top, between the third and fourth row in A above the last stripe in B; work the running stitches over one sc and under one sc alternately.

Using D, work a second line of running stitches in the same way all around the top, two rows above first line of running stitches.

SNAIL MOTIF (optional)

SNAIL'S SHELL Ⓐ

Using size C-2 (2.5mm) hook and C, ch 4 and join with a sl st to first ch to form a ring.

Round 1 (RS) Ch 1, 8 sc in ring, change to B and join with a sl st to first sc. *8 sc.*

(Do not turn at end of rounds, but work with RS always facing.)

Round 2 Using B, ch 1, 2 sc in each sc to end of round, change to D and join with a sl st to first sc. *16 sc.*

Round 3 Using D, ch 1, [2 sc in next sc, 1 sc in next sc] 8 times, change to B and join with a sl st to first sc. *24 sc.*

Round 4 Using B, ch 1, [2 sc in next sc, 1 sc in each of next 2 sc] 8 times, change to C and join with a sl st to first sc. *32 sc.*

Round 5 Using C, ch 1, [2 sc in next sc, 1 sc in each of next 3 sc] 8 times, join with a sl st to first sc. *40 sc.*

Fasten off.

SNAIL'S BODY Ⓑ

Using size C-2 (2.5mm) hook and B, ch 18.

Foundation row (RS) 1 sl st in 2nd ch from hook, 1 sl st in next ch, 1 sc in next ch, 1 hdc in each of next 2 ch, 1 dc in each of next 3 ch, 1 hdc in next ch, 1 sc in next ch, 1 sl st in each of next 2 ch, 1 sc in each of last 5 ch.

Fasten off.

TO FINISH

Sew snail's shell and body to front just above top line of running stitches and under right shoulder, positioning top of foundation row of body along belly of snail as shown.

Using a blunt-ended yarn needle and B, work a couched line for each of the snail's antenna as shown. Sew a button to top of each antenna.

LITTLE STRIPY BAG

Very simple and very stylish, this Little Stripy Bag is useful for keeping all your favorite things in. Make the strap long enough to go over your head or short to use as a handbag—whatever suits you!

SIZE

The finished bag measures approximately 6¾in/17cm wide by 6¾in/17cm deep.

YARN

Rowan 4-Ply Soft (1¾oz/50g balls) as follows:

A sage green (Leafy 367)	1 ball
B pale blue (Whisper 370)	1 ball
C red (Honk 374)	1 ball

HOOK

Size C-2 (2.5mm) crochet hook

GAUGE

25 sts and 26 rows to 4in/10cm measured over sc using size C-2 (2.5mm) crochet hook or *size necessary to obtain correct gauge.*

ABBREVIATIONS

See page 110.

MAIN SECTION OF BAG

The main section of the bag is worked in one piece that is folded in half to form the bag.
Using size C-2 (2.5mm) hook and A, ch 69.
Foundation row (RS) 1 sc in 2nd ch from hook, 1 sc in each of rem ch, turn. *68 sc.*
Row 1 (patt row) Ch 1 (does NOT count as a st), 1 sc in each sc to end, turn.
(Last row forms simple sc patt when repeated.)
Cont in sc throughout, **work 2 rows B, 2 rows A, 2 rows C, and 2 rows A.**
Rep from ** to ** 4 times more (a total of 42 rows worked from beg).

Work 2 rows B, 2 rows A (a total of 46 rows worked from beg).
Fasten off.

TO FINISH

Press main section of bag lightly on wrong side, following instructions on yarn label.

Top borders (both alike)
With RS facing and using size C-2 (2.5mm) hook and A, work top border along each side-edge of main section as follows:
Row 1 (RS) Join A with a sl st to first row-end, ch 1 (does NOT count as a st), 1 sc in same place as sl st, *1 sc in each of rem row-ends, turn. 46 sc.
Row 2 Ch 1, 1 sc in each sc to end, turn.
Rep last row 5 times more, ending with a RS row.
Fasten off.
Fold main section in half widthwise with right sides together and sew side seams. Turn right-side out.

Edging
With RS facing and using size C-2 (2.5mm) hook and C, work edging along top of bag as follows:
Round 1 (RS) Join C with a sl st to a sc at side seam, ch 2 (to count as first sc and first 1-ch sp), skip next sc, *1 sc in next sc, ch 1, skip next sc; rep from * all around top of bag, join with a sl st to first of 2-ch.
Fasten off.
With RS facing, join in B on next round as follows:
Round 2 (RS) Join B with a sl st to last 1-ch sp of last round, ch 2 (to count as first sc and first 1-ch sp), *1 sc in next 1-ch sp, ch 1; rep from * end of round, join with a sl st to first of 2-ch.
Fasten off.
With RS facing, join in A and work next round as for round 2.
Fasten off.

Bag strap
Make a twisted cord for bag strap as follows:
Cut four strands of A, each approximately

3¼yd/3m long. Align the strands and knot them together at each end. Hook one end over a door handle, and insert a pencil through the other end. Twist pencil clockwise until strands are tightly twisted. Holding cord in center with one hand, bring ends together and let two halves twist together.

Knot each end to make a finished strap 42½in/ 108cm long. Trim ends close to knots.

Starting at one corner at bottom edge of bag, sew ends of cord to inside of bag all along side seams.

BON-BON BLANKET

This very special little Bon-Bon Blanket with its dainty circles in candy stripes is surprisingly easy to make—all you need to do is work simple rounds of double crochet. Once it's made, enjoy it all the more by sharing it with a friend.

BEFORE YOU BEGIN

SIZE

The finished blanket measures approximately 36½in/93cm wide by 46in/117cm long, including the edging.

Note: To make a smaller or bigger blanket, simply make fewer or more circles.

YARN

Rowan *4-Ply Soft* (1¾oz/50g balls) as follows:

A pink (Fairy 395)		7 balls
B red (Honk 374)		6 balls
C sage green (Leafy 367)		2 balls
D sea green (Folly 391)		2 balls

HOOK

Size C-2 (2.5mm) crochet hook

GAUGE

Each large circle measures 2⅜in/6cm in diameter using a size C-2 (2.5mm) crochet hook *or size necessary to obtain correct gauge.*

ABBREVIATIONS

sc2tog = [insert hook in next st, yo and draw a loop through] twice, yo and draw through all 3 loops on hook—*one st decreased.*
See also page 110.

GETTING STARTED

LARGE CIRCLE 1 (make 143)

Using size C-2 (2.5mm) hook and A, ch 6 and join with a sl st to first ch to form a ring.

Round 1 (RS) Using A, ch 3 (to count as first dc), 15 dc in ring, change to B and join with a sl st to 3rd of 3-ch. *16 sts.*
(Do not turn at end of rounds, but work with RS always facing.)

Round 2 Using B, ch 3, 1 dc in same place as last sl st, 2 dc in each dc to end of round, change to A and join with a sl st to 3rd of 3-ch. *32 sts.* Cut off B.

Round 3 Using A, ch 3, 1 dc in same place as last sl st, 1 dc in next dc, *2 dc in next dc, 1 dc in next dc; rep from * to end of round, join with a sl st in 3rd of 3-ch. *48 sts.*
Fasten off, leaving a long tail-end of yarn.

LARGE CIRCLE 2 (make 142)

Work as for Large Circle 1, but use B in place of A, and A in place of B.

SMALL CIRCLE 1 (make 126)

Using size C-2 (2.5mm) hook and C, ch 6 and join with a sl st to first ch to form a ring.

Round 1 (RS) Ch 3 (to count as first dc), 15 dc in ring, join with a sl st to 3rd of 3-ch. *16 sts.*
Fasten off, leaving a long tail-end of yarn.

SMALL CIRCLE 2 (make 126)

Work as for Small Circle 1, but use D instead of C.

TO FINISH

Arrange all large circles in a rectangle 15 circles wide by 19 circles long, with a Large Circle 1 at each of four corners and alternating Large Circles 1 and 2 (see below).

Using long tail-ends of yarn, sew together large

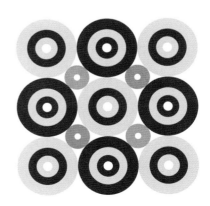

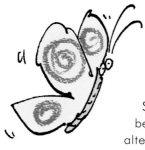

circles by stitching together 3 dc where circles touch (and leaving 9 dc free between each 3-dc joining point). Sew small circles into spaces between large circles, alternating Small Circles 1 and 2.

Edging

With RS facing and using size C-2 (2.5mm) hook, work edging around blanket as follows:

Round 1 (RS) Using D, join yarn with a sl st to a corner dc, ch 1 (does NOT count as a st), 1 sc in same place as sl st, *1 sc in each dc to 1 dc before 3-dc joining point, work sc2tog over next dc and first free dc on next circle; rep from * all around edge of blanket, 1 sc in each dc to end of round, join with a sl st to first sc.
Fasten off.
(Do not turn at end of rounds, but work with RS always facing.)

Round 2 Using C, join yarn with a sl st to same place as last sl st, ch 1, 1 sc in same place as sl st, *1 sc in each sc to 1 sc before sc2tog, then insert hook in next sc, yo and draw a loop through, skip next st (which is top of sc2tog) and insert hook in next sc, yo and draw a loop through, yo and draw through all 3 loops on hook to complete sc2tog; rep from * all around, 1 sc in each sc to end of round, join with a sl st to first sc.
Fasten off.

Round 3 Using A, rep round 2.
Fasten off.

Round 4 Using B, rep round 2.
Fasten off.

Round 5 Using A, join yarn with a sl st to same place as last sl st, ch 1, 1 sc in same place as sl st, 1 sc in each sc to end.
Fasten off.

Press lightly on wrong side, following instructions on yarn label.

SWEET CICELY SKIRT

This gorgeous skirt is easily made in a simple textured stitch. It is Sweet Cicely's favorite and is really comfortable to wear with pretty pockets, edgings, and buttons. When worn with the Sweet Cicely Top (see page 34), it makes a fantastic outfit. The Summer Cap and Best Beach Bag (see pages 38 and 49) complement it perfectly. Sweet Cicely really does look very sweet, doesn't she!

SIZES AND MEASUREMENTS

To fit ages (in years)	2–3	3–4	4–5
Finished measurements			
Length to waist	10¼ in	12¼ in	14¼ in
	26cm	31cm	36cm

YARN

Rowan *4-Ply Cotton* (1¾ oz/50g balls) as follows:

		2–3	3–4	4–5
A	pale green (Fresh 131)	3 balls	4 balls	4 balls
B	mid green (Fennel 135)	1 ball	1 ball	1 ball

Rowan *Cotton Glace* (1¾ oz/50g balls) as follows:

		2–3	3–4	4–5
C	red (Poppy 741)	1 ball	1 ball	1 ball

HOOKS

Size C-2 (2.5mm) crochet hook
Size D-3 (3mm) crochet hook

EXTRAS

2 red buttons ¾ in/18mm in diameter, for pocket flaps

GAUGE

30 sts and 18 rows to 4in/10cm measured over patt using A and size D-3 (3mm) crochet hook *or size necessary to obtain correct gauge.*

ABBREVIATIONS

sc2tog = [insert hook in next st, yo and draw a loop through] twice, yo and draw through all 3 loops on hook—*one st decreased.*
See also page 110.

FRONT OF SKIRT

Using size D-3 (3mm) hook and A, ch 131 (145: 163).

Foundation row (RS) 1 sc and 1 hdc in 3rd ch from hook, *skip next ch, 1 sc and 1 hdc in next ch; rep from * to end, turn. *130 (144: 162) sts.*

Row 1 (patt row) Ch 2 (does NOT count as a st), 1 sc and 1 hdc in first hdc, *1 sc and 1 hdc in next hdc; rep from * to end, turn.

(Last row forms patt when repeated.)

Work 0 (2: 6) rows more in patt, ending with a WS row.

Next row (dec row) (RS) Ch 2, 1 sc and 1 hdc in first hdc, [1 sc and 1 hdc in next hdc] 9 times, 1 sc in next hdc, 1 hdc in next hdc, work in patt to last 24 sts, 1 sc in next hdc, 1 hdc in next hdc, [1 sc and 1 hdc in next hdc] 10 times, turn. *(4 sts decreased.)*

Work even in patt for 3 rows.

Rep last 4 rows 8 (9: 11) times more and then the dec row again. 90 *(100: 110) sts.*

Work even in patt until Front measures 9½ (11½ : 13½) in/24 (29: 34) cm from beg, ending with a RS row.

Next row (WS) Ch 1 (does NOT count as a st), 1 sc in each st to end, turn. 90 *(100: 110) sc.*

Cut off A.

Waistband

Change to size C-2 (2.5mm) hook and B and work waistband as follows:

Next row (dec row) (RS) Ch 1, 1 sc in each of first 2 (7: 12) sc, work sc2tog over next 2 sc, [1 sc in next sc, work sc2tog over next 2 sc] 28 times, 1 sc in each of last 2 (7: 12) sc, turn. *61 (71: 81) sc.*

Next row Ch 1, 1 sc in each sc to end, turn.
Rep last row twice more.

Next row (eyelet row) (RS) Ch 1, 1 sc in each of first 2 sc, *ch 3, skip next 2 sc, 1 sc in each of next 3 sc; rep from * to last 4 sc, ch 3, skip next 2 sc, 1 sc in each of last 2 sc, turn.

Next row Ch 1, 1 sc in each of first 2 sc, *2 sc in next 3-ch sp, 1 sc in each of next 3 sc; rep from *

to last 3-ch sp, 2 sc in next 3-ch sp, 1 sc in each of last 2 sc, turn.

Next row Ch 1, 1 sc in each sc to end.

Fasten off.

BACK OF SKIRT

Work exactly as for Front of Skirt.

POCKETS (make 2)

Using size D-3 (3mm) hook and A, ch 23.

Foundation row (RS) 1 sc and 1 hdc in 3rd ch from hook, *skip next ch, 1 sc and 1 hdc in next ch; rep from * to end, turn. 22 sts.

Row 1 (patt row) Ch 2 (does NOT count as a st), 1 sc and 1 hdc in first hdc, *1 sc and 1 hdc in next hdc; rep from * to end, turn.

(Last row forms patt when repeated.)

Work even in patt for 12 rows, ending with a WS row.

Pocket flap

Next row (RS of pocket, WS of flap) Ch 1 (does NOT count as a st), 1 sc in each st to end, turn. 22 sc.

Next row (dec row) Ch 1, 1 sc in first sc, work sc2tog over next 2 sc, 1 sc in each sc to last 3 sc, work sc2tog over next 2 sc, 1 sc in last sc, turn.

Rep last row 7 times more. 6 sc.

Next row Ch 1, 1 sc in first sc, [work sc2tog over next 2 sc] twice, 1 sc in last sc, turn. 4 sc.

Next row Ch 1, [work sc2tog over next 2 sc] twice. 2 sc.

Fasten off.

Pocket edging

With RS of pocket flap (and WS of pocket) facing and using size C-2 (2.5mm) hook and B, work edging along edge of shaped pocket flap as follows:

Row 1 (RS) Join B with a sl st to first row-end at beg of side-edge of flap, ch 1, 1 sc in same place as sl st, skip next row-end, [3 dc and 1 sl st in next row-end, 1 sc in next row-end, skip next row-end] 3 times, 3 dc and 1 sl st in center of top of last row of flap, then cont along other side of flap and skip first row-end, [1 sc in next row-end, 3 dc and 1 sl st in next row-end, skip next row-end] 3 times, 1 sc in last row-end. Fasten off.

TO FINISH

Press pieces lightly on wrong side, following instructions on yarn label.

Fold each pocket flap to right side of pocket and secure in place with a button. Sew pockets to Front of Skirt as shown on opposite page. Sew Front and Back of skirt together along side edges.

Skirt-hem edging

With RS facing and using size C-2 (2.5mm) hook and B, work edging along foundation-chain edge of skirt as follows:

Round 1 (RS) Join B with a sl st to 1-ch sp at a side seam, ch 1, 1 sc in same place as sl st, *3 dc and 1 sl st in next ch sp, 1 sc in next ch sp; rep from * to last ch sp, 3 dc in last ch sp, join with a sl st to first sc.

Fasten off.

Drawstring

Using size C-2 (2.5mm) hook and C and leaving a long tail-end (about 39½in/100cm long), make a ch long enough to fit around waist and tie neatly (approximately 28½in/72cm long), then work 10 dc in 3rd ch from hook to form a bobble at end of chain.

Fasten off, thread this tail-end of yarn through top of dc, pull up tightly to complete the bobble and secure.

Beginning at center front, thread drawstring through eyelet holes in waistband. Then work a bobble in the same way as the first bobble at the other end of the drawstring, using the long tail-end at beginning of foundation chain.

33

SWEET CICELY TOP

The Sweet Cicely Top is just the thing to wear on a warm summer's day at the beach. It is easily made in simple single and half double crochet. The cotton yarn will keep you cool and the lovely little cap sleeves will keep the sun off delicate shoulders. Slip it on and splash about.

BEFORE YOU BEGIN

SIZES AND MEASUREMENTS

To fit ages (in years)	2–3	3–4	4–5
To fit chest	22in	24in	26in
	56cm	61cm	66cm
Finished measurements			
Around chest	27in	29½in	31½in
	69cm	75cm	80cm
Length to shoulder	11¾in	12½in	13½in
	30cm	32cm	34cm

YARN

Rowan *4-Ply Cotton* (1¾oz/50g balls) as follows:

A	mid green (Fennel 135)	2 balls	3 balls	3 balls
B	pale green (Fresh 131)	1 ball	1 ball	1 ball

Rowan *Cotton Glace* (1¾oz/50g balls) as follows:

C	red (Poppy 741)	1 ball	1 ball	1 ball

HOOKS

Size C-2 (2.5mm) crochet hook
Size D-3 (3mm) crochet hook

GAUGE

23 hdc and 18 rows to 4in/10cm measured over hdc using A and size D-3 (3mm) crochet hook or *size necessary to obtain correct gauge.*
23 sc and 26 rows to 4in/10cm measured over sc using A and size D-3 (3mm) crochet hook or *size necessary to obtain correct gauge.*

ABBREVIATIONS

sc2tog = [insert hook in next st, yo and draw a loop through] twice, yo and draw through all 3 loops on hook—*one st decreased.*
hdc2tog = [yo and insert hook in next st, yo and draw a loop through] twice, yo and draw through all 5 loops on hook—*one st decreased.* See also page 110.

GETTING STARTED

BACK

Using size D-3 (3mm) hook and A, ch 91 (97: 103).

Foundation row (RS) 1 hdc in 3rd ch from hook, 1 hdc in each of rem ch, turn. 90 (96: 102) sts.
Row 1 (patt row) Ch 2 (to count as first hdc), skip first hdc, 1 hdc in each hdc to end, 1 hdc in 2nd of 2-ch, turn.
(Last row forms simple hdc patt when repeated.)
Cont in hdc, work 2 rows more in A and 2 rows in B, ending with a WS row.
Next row (dec row) (RS) Using A, ch 2, skip first hdc, 1 dc in each of next 4 hdc, work hdc2tog over next 2 hdc, 1 hdc in each hdc to last 6 hdc, work hdc2tog over next 2 hdc, 1 dc in each of next 4 hdc, 1 hdc in 2nd of 2-ch, turn.
Cont in hdc, work 1 row more in A and 2 rows in B.
Rep last 4 rows 4 times more, ending with a WS row. 80 (86: 92) sts.
Cut off B and cont in A only.
Next row (RS) Ch 1 (does NOT count as a st), 1 sc in first hdc, 1 sc in each hdc to end, 1 sc in 2nd of 2-ch, turn. 80 (86: 92) sc.
Next row Ch 1, 1 sc in each sc to end, turn.
Rep last row until Back measures 6¾ (7: 7½)in/ 17 (18: 19)cm from beg, ending with a RS row.

Shape armholes

Next row (WS) 1 sl st in each of first 5 sc, ch 1, 1 sc in same sc as last sl st, 1 sc in each sc to last 4 sc, turn. 72 (78: 84) sc.**
Next row Ch 1, 1 sc in first sc, work sc2tog over next 2 sc, 1 sc in each sc to last 3 sc, work sc2tog over next 2 sc, 1 sc in last sc, turn.
Rep last row 19 (21: 23) times more, ending with a WS row. 32 (34: 36) sc.
Fasten off.

FRONT

Work as for Back to **.

Next row (RS) Ch 1, 1 sc in first sc, work sc2tog over next 2 sc, 1 sc in each sc to last 3 sc, work sc2tog over next 2 sc, 1 sc in last sc, turn.

Rep last row 9 (11: 13) times more, ending with a WS row. 52 (54: 56) sc.

Divide for front neck opening

Next row (RS) Ch 1, 1 sc in first sc, work sc2tog over next 2 sc, 1 sc in each of next 23 (24: 25) sc, turn. 25 (26: 27) sc.

Working on these sts only for first side of neck opening, cont as follows:

Next row Ch 1, 1 sc in each sc to last 3 sc, work sc2tog over next 2 sc, 1 sc in last sc, turn.

Next row Ch 1, 1 sc in first sc, work sc2tog over next 2 sc, 1 sc in each sc to end, turn.

Next row Ch 1, 1 sc in each sc to last 3 sc, work sc2tog over next 2 sc, 1 sc in last sc, turn.

Rep last 2 rows 3 times more, ending with a WS row. 16 (17: 18) sc.

Fasten off.

With RS facing, return to sts left unworked and rejoin A with a sl st to next sc, ch 1, 1 sc in same sc as sl st, 1 sc in each sc to last 3 sc, work sc2tog over next 2 sc, 1 sc in last sc, turn.

Next row Ch 1, 1 sc in first sc, work sc2tog over next 2 sc, 1 sc in each sc to end, turn.

Next row Ch 1, 1 sc in each sc to last 3 sc, work sc2tog over next 2 sc, 1 sc in last sc, turn.

Next row Ch 1, 1 sc in first sc, work sc2tog over next 2 sc, 1 sc in each sc to end, turn.

Rep last 2 rows 3 times more, ending with a WS row. 16 (17: 18) sc.

Do NOT fasten off, but leave this ball of A at neck edge to work neck edging later.

SLEEVES (make 2)

Using size D-3 (3mm) hook and A, ch 66 (71: 76).

Foundation row (RS) 1 sc in 2nd ch from hook, 1 sc in each of rem ch, turn. 65 (70: 75) sc.

Row 1 (patt row) Ch 1 (does NOT count as a st), 1 sc in each sc to end, turn.

(Last row forms simple sc patt when repeated.)

Next row (inc row) Ch 1, 1 sc in each of first 3 sc, 2 sc in next sc, 1 sc in each sc to last 4 sc, 2 sc in next sc, 1 sc in each of last 3 sc, turn.

Cont in sc throughout, work even for 2 rows.

Rep last 3 rows 0 (1: 2) times more. 67 (74: 81) sc.

Next row (inc row) Ch 1, 1 sc in each of first 3 sc, 2 sc in next sc, 1 sc in each sc to last 4 sc, 2 sc in next sc, 1 sc in each of last 3 sc, turn. 69 (76: 83) sc.

Work even for 3 (2: 1) rows.

Shape top of sleeve

Next row 1 sl st in each of first 5 sc, ch 1, 1 sc in same sc as last sl st, 1 sc in each sc to last 4 sc, turn. 61 (68: 75) sc.

Next row Ch 1, 1 sc in first sc, work sc2tog over next 2 sc, 1 sc in each sc to last 3 sc, work sc2tog over next 2 sc, 1 sc in last sc, turn.

Rep last row 19 (21: 23) times more. 21 (24: 27) sc.

Fasten off.

TO FINISH

Press pieces lightly on wrong side, following instructions on yarn label.

Sew sleeves to Back and Front along raglan edges.

Neck edging

With RS facing and using size D-3 (3mm) hook, pick up A left at beg of neck edge on right front and cont as follows:

Row 1 (RS) Ch 1, 1 sc in each of first 15 (16: 17) sc, work sc2tog over last sc of front neck edge and first sc of right sleeve neck edge, 1 sc in each of next 19 (22: 25) sc, work sc2tog over last sc of sleeve neck edge and first sc of back neck edge, 1 sc in each of next 14 (15: 16) sc, work sc2tog over next 2 sc, 1 sc in each of next 14 (15: 16) sc, work sc2tog over last sc of back neck edge and first sc of left sleeve neck edge, 1 sc in each of next 19 (22: 25) sc, work sc2tog over last sc of sleeve neck edge and first sc of left front neck edge, 1 sc in each sc to end, turn. 101 (111: 121) sc.

Row 2 Ch 1, 1 sc in each sc to end, turn.

Row 3 (eyelet row) Ch 1, 1 sc in each of first 2 sc, *ch 3, skip next 2 sc, 1 sc in each of next 3 sc; rep from * to last 4 sc, ch 3, skip next 2 sc, 1 sc in each of last 2 sc, turn.

Row 4 Ch 1, 1 sc in each of first 2 sc, *2 sc in next 3-ch sp, 1 sc in each of next 3 sc; rep from * to last 3-ch sp, 2 sc in next 3-ch sp, 1 sc in each of next 2 sc, turn.

Row 5 Ch 1, 1 sc in each sc to end. Fasten off.

Hem edging

Sew side and sleeve seams.

With RS facing and using size C-2 (2.5mm) hook and A, work edging along foundation-chain edge of top as follows:

Round 1 (RS) Join A with a sl st to first ch of foundation-chain edge of top at a side seam, 1 sc in same place as sl st, *skip 1 ch, [3 dc, 1 sl st] all in next ch, skip 1 ch, 1 sc in next ch; rep from * to last 3 ch, skip 1 ch, [3 dc, 1 sl st] all in next ch, join with a sl st to first sc.
Fasten off.

Sleeve edging

With RS facing and using size C-2 (2.5mm) hook and A, work edging along edge of sleeve as follows:

Round 1 (RS) Join A with a sl st to first ch of foundation-chain edge of sleeve at side seam, 1 sc in same place as sl st, *skip 2 ch, [3 dc, 1 sl st] all in next ch, skip 1 ch, 1 sc in next ch; rep from * to last 3 ch, skip 1 ch, [3 dc, 1 sl st] all in next ch, join with a sl st to first sc.
Fasten off.

Drawstring

Using size C-2 (2.5mm) hook and C and leaving a long tail-end (about 39½in/100cm long), make a ch long enough to fit around neck and tie neatly (approximately 22in/56cm long), then work 10 dc in 3rd ch from hook to form a bobble at end of chain.

Fasten off, thread this tail-end of yarn through top of dc, pull up tightly to complete the bobble and secure.

Beginning at center front neck opening, thread drawstring chain through eyelet holes in neck edging. Then work a bobble in the same way as the first bobble at the other end of the drawstring, using the long tail-end at beginning of foundation chain.

Fold front corners of neck edge down as shown below and secure in place with a couple of hand stitches.

Tie drawstring ends together at center front neck.

SUMMER CAP

This cap is simple and quick to make in easy double crochet. Keep it plain for boys and brightly decorated for girls. Not only is it perfect for keeping unruly curls in place on a breezy day, but it will lend a certain "je-ne-sais-quoi" to any outfit.

BEFORE YOU BEGIN

SIZES AND MEASUREMENTS

To fit ages (in years)	2–3	3–4	4–5
Finished hat measurements			
Circumference	17in	18in	19in
	43cm	46cm	48cm
Length from center top	6½in	6¾in	7in
	16cm	17cm	18cm

YARN

Pale Green Cap
Rowan *4-Ply Cotton* (1¾oz/50g balls) as follows:

A pale green (Fresh 131)	1 ball	1 ball	1 ball
B turquoise (Aegean 129)	1 ball	1 ball	1 ball

Rowan *Cotton Glace* (1¾oz/50g balls) as follows:

C red (Poppy 741)	1 ball	1 ball	1 ball

Mid Green Cap
Rowan *4-Ply Cotton* (1¾oz/50g balls) as follows:

A mid green (Fennel 135)	1 ball	1 ball	1 ball
B pale green (Fresh 131)	1 ball	1 ball	1 ball

Rowan *Cotton Glace* (1¾oz/50g balls) as follows:

C red (Poppy 741)	1 ball	1 ball	1 ball

Blue Cap
Rowan *4-Ply Cotton* (1¾oz/50g balls) as follows:

A navy (Navy 150)	1 ball	1 ball	1 ball
B turquoise (Aegean 129)	1 ball	1 ball	1 ball

HOOKS
Size D-3 (3mm) crochet hook
Size C-2 (2.5mm) crochet hook

GAUGE
23 dc and 13 rows to 4in/10cm measured over dc using A and size D-3 (3mm) crochet hook *or size necessary to obtain correct gauge.*

ABBREVIATIONS
See page 110.

GETTING STARTED

PALE GREEN CAP

TO MAKE CAP
Using size D-3 (3mm) hook and A, ch 6 and join with a sl st to first ch to form a ring.

Round 1 (RS) Ch 3 (to count as first dc), 15 dc in ring, join with a sl st to 3rd of 3-ch, turn. *16 sts.*
(**Note:** First 3-ch of each round counts as first dc. Remember to turn at the end of each round.)

Round 2 Ch 3, 1 dc in same place as sl st, 2 dc in each dc to end, join with a sl st to 3rd of 3-ch, turn. *32 sts.*

Round 3 Ch 3, 1 dc in each dc to end, join with a sl st to 3rd of 3-ch, turn.

Round 4 Ch 3, 2 dc in next dc, [1 dc in next dc, 2 dc in next dc] 15 times, join with a sl st to 3rd of 3-ch, turn. *48 sts.*

Round 5 Ch 3, 1 dc in next dc, 2 dc in next dc, [1 dc in each of next 2 dc, 2 dc in next dc] 15 times, join with a sl st to 3rd of 3-ch, turn. *64 sts.*

Round 6 Ch 3, 1 dc in each dc to end, join with a sl st to 3rd of 3-ch, turn.

Round 7 Ch 3, 1 dc in each of next 2 dc, 2 dc in next dc, [1 dc in each of next 3 dc, 2 dc in next dc] 15 times, join with a sl st to 3rd of 3-ch, turn. *80 sts.*

Round 8 Ch 3, 1 dc in each of next 2 dc, 2 dc in next dc, [1 dc in each of next 3 dc, 2 dc in next dc] 19 times, join with a sl st to 3rd of 3-ch, turn. *100 sts.*

1st size only:
Round 9 Ch 3, 1 dc in each dc to end, join with a sl st to 3rd of 3-ch, turn. *100 sts.*

2nd size only:
Round 9 Ch 3, 1 dc in each of next 18 dc, 2 dc in next dc, [1 dc in each of next 19 dc, 2 dc in next dc] 4 times, join with a sl st to 3rd of 3-ch, turn. *105 sts.*

3rd size only:
Round 9 Ch 3, 1 dc in each of next 8 dc, 2 dc in next dc, [1 dc in each of next 9 dc, 2 dc in next dc] 9 times, join with a sl st to 3rd of 3-ch, turn. *110 sts.*

All sizes:

Round 10 Ch 3, 1 dc in each dc to end, join with a sl st to 3rd of 3-ch, turn.

Rep last round 11 (12: 13) times more. Fasten off.

DECORATIVE DOUBLE RINGS (make 7)

Using size C-2 (2.5mm) hook and B, ch 12 and join with a sl st to first ch to form a ring.

Round 1 Ch 3 (to count as first dc), 11 dc in ring, join with a sl st to 3rd of 3-ch. Fasten off to complete first section of double ring.

Using size C-2 (2.5mm) crochet hook and C, ch 12, pass hook through first section of double ring and join with a sl st to first ch to form a ring linked around first ring.

Round 1 Ch 3 (to count as first dc), 11 dc in ring, join with a sl st to 3rd of 3-ch. Fasten off to complete double ring. Make 6 more double rings in same way.

TO FINISH

Press pieces lightly on wrong side, following instructions on yarn label.

Cap edging

With RS facing and using size C-2 (2.5mm) hook and C, work edging along last row of cap as follows:

Round 1 (RS) Join C with a sl st to any dc, ch 1, 1 sc in same place as sl st, 1 sc in each st to end, join with a sl st to first sc. Fasten off.

Decorative double rings

Sew rings to cap, equally spaced and about ¾in/2cm from edge.

MID GREEN CAP

TO MAKE CAP
Make and finish as for Pale Green Cap.

BLUE CAP

TO MAKE CAP
Make and finish as for Pale Green Cap, but omitting decorative double rings and working cap edging in B.

WILBUR WHALE

Wilbur Whale loves the deep blue sea and is incredibly happy down there swimming about. There is nothing complicated about making Wilbur as he is made in three simple pieces in single crochet with easy embroidery and little button eyes.

BEFORE YOU BEGIN

SIZE
The finished toy whale measures approximately 8¾in/22cm long by 4½in/11.5cm tall.

YARN
Blue Whale
Rowan *4-Ply Cotton* (1¾oz/50g balls) as follows:
A navy (Navy 150)   1 ball
B turquoise (Aegean 129)   1 ball
Rowan *Cotton Glace* (1¾oz/50g balls) as follows:
C red (Poppy 741)   small amount
Turquoise Whale
Rowan *4-Ply Cotton* (1¾oz/50g balls) as follows:
A turquoise (Aegean 129)   1 ball
B navy (Navy 150)   1 ball
Rowan *Cotton Glace* (1¾oz/50g balls) as follows:
C red (Poppy 741)   small amount

HOOK
Size C-2 (2.5mm) crochet hook

EXTRAS
Washable stuffing
2 buttons ⁷⁄₁₆in/11mm in diameter, for eyes

GAUGE
23 sts and 30 rows to 4in/10cm measured over sc using A and size C-2 (2.5mm) crochet hook *or size necessary to obtain correct gauge.*

ABBREVIATIONS
sc2tog = [insert hook in next st, yo and draw a loop through] twice, yo and draw through all 3 loops on hook—*one st decreased.*
See also page 110.

GETTING STARTED

BODY—LEFT SIDE Ⓐ
Each side of the whale's body is worked from the front end to the tail.
Using size C-2 (2.5mm) hook and A, ch 27.
Foundation row (RS) 1 sc in 2nd ch from hook, 1 sc in each of rem ch, turn. *26 sc.*
Row 1 Ch 1 (does NOT count as a st), 2 sc in first sc, 1 sc in each sc to last 2 sc, 2 sc in each of last 2 sc, turn. *29 sc.*
To help keep track of which is RS of piece, after turning work and before beg next row, mark this side of work as RS with a colored thread.
Row 2 (RS) Ch 1, 2 sc in first sc, 1 sc in each sc to last sc, 2 sc in last sc, turn. *31 sc.*
Row 3 Ch 1, 1 sc in each sc to end, turn.
Row 4 Ch 1, 1 sc in each sc to last sc, 2 sc in last sc, turn. *32 sc.*
Row 5 Ch 1, 1 sc in each sc to end, turn.
Rows 6–48 [Rep row 5] 43 times.
Row 49 Ch 1, work sc2tog over first 2 sc, 1 sc in each sc to end, turn. *31 sc.*
Row 50 Rep row 5.
Row 51 Rep row 49. *30 sc.*
Row 52 Ch 1, 1 sc in each sc to last 2 sc, work sc2tog over last 2 sc, turn. *29 sc.*
Row 53 Ch 1, work sc2tog over first 2 sc, 1 sc in each sc to last 4 sc, [work sc2tog over next 2 sc] twice, turn. *26 sc.*
Row 54 Ch 1, skip first sc, [work sc2tog over next 2 sc] twice, 1 sc in each sc to last 4 sc, [work sc2tog over next 2 sc] twice, turn. *21 sc.*
Row 55 Ch 1, [work sc2tog over next 2 sc] twice, 1 sc in each sc to last 4 sc, [work sc2tog over next 2 sc] twice, turn. *17 sc.*
Fasten off.

Shape tail
With RS facing, work tail by rejoining A to sts as follows:
Row 56 (RS) Skip first 7 sc and rejoin A with a sl st to next sc, ch 1, 1 sc in same place as sl st, 1 sc in each of next 3 sc, turn. *4 sc.*
Row 57 Ch 1, 2 sc in first sc, 1 sc in each sc to

last sc, 2 sc in last sc, turn. 6 *sc.*
Rows 58–66 [Rep row 57] 9 times. 24 *sc.*
Fasten off.

BODY—RIGHT SIDE 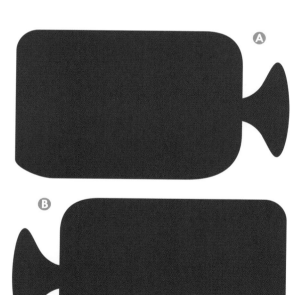 B

Using size C-2 (2.5mm) hook and A, ch 27.
Foundation row (RS) 1 sc in 2nd ch from hook,
1 sc in each of rem ch, turn. 26 *sc.*
Row 1 Ch 1 (does NOT count as a st), 2 sc in
each of first 2 sc, 1 sc in each sc to last sc, 2 sc in
last sc, turn. 29 *sc.*
To help keep track of which is RS of piece, after
turning work and before beg next row, mark this
side of work as RS with a colored thread.
Row 2 (RS) Ch 1, 2 sc in first sc, 1 sc in each sc
to last sc, 2 sc in last sc, turn. 31 *sc.*
Row 3 Ch 1, 1 sc in each sc to end, turn.
Row 4 Ch 1, 2 sc in first sc, 1 sc in each sc to
end, turn. 32 *sc.*
Row 5 Ch 1, 1 sc in each sc to end, turn.

Rows 6–48 [Rep row 5] 43 times.
Row 49 Ch 1, 1 sc in each sc to last 2 sc, work
sc2tog over last 2 sc, turn. 31 *sc.*
Row 50 Rep row 5.
Row 51 Rep row 49. 30 *sc.*
Row 52 Ch 1, work sc2tog over first 2 sc, 1 sc in
each sc to end, turn. 29 *sc.*
Row 53 Ch 1, [work sc2tog over next 2 sc]
twice, 1 sc in each sc to last 2 sc, work sc2tog
over last 2 sc, turn. 26 *sc.*
Row 54 Ch 1, [work sc2tog over next 2 sc]
twice, 1 sc in each sc to last 5 sc, work sc2tog
over next 2 sc, work sc2tog over next sc and last
sc (skipping sc in between), turn. 21 *sc.*
Row 55 Ch 1, [work sc2tog over next 2 sc]
twice, 1 sc in each sc to last 4 sc, [work sc2tog
over next 2 sc] twice, turn. 17 *sc.*
Fasten off.

Shape tail

With RS facing, work tail by rejoining A to sts as
follows:
Row 56 (RS) Skip first 6 sc and rejoin A with a
sl st to next sc, ch 1, 1 sc in same place as sl st,
1 sc in each of next 3 sc, turn. 4 *sc.*
Row 57 Ch 1, 2 sc in first sc, 1 sc in each sc to
last sc, 2 sc in last sc, turn. 6 *sc.*
Rows 58–66 [Rep row 57] 9 times. 24 *sc.*
Fasten off.

UNDERBODY 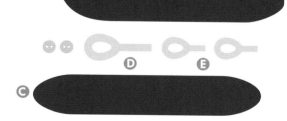 C

The underbody of the whale is worked from the
mouth to the tail-end of the whale.
Using size C-2 (2.5mm) hook and A, ch 3.
Foundation row (RS) 1 sc in 2nd ch from hook,
1 sc in last ch, turn. 2 *sc.*
Row 1 Ch 1 (does NOT count as a st), 2 sc in
first sc, 2 sc in last sc, turn. 4 *sc.*
Row 2 Ch 1, 2 sc in first sc, 1 sc in each sc to last
sc, 2 sc in last sc, turn. 6 *sc.*
Row 3 Ch 1, 1 sc in each sc to end, turn.
Row 4 Ch 1, 2 sc in first sc, 1 sc in each sc to last
sc, 2 sc in last sc, turn. 8 *sc.*
Row 5 Ch 1, 1 sc in each sc to end, turn.
Rows 6–48 [Rep row 5] 43 times.
Row 49 Ch 1, work sc2tog over first 2 sc, 1 sc in
each sc to last 2 sc, work sc2tog over last 2 sc,
turn. 6 *sc.*

Row 50 Rep row 5.
Row 51 Rep row 49. *4 sc.*
Row 52 Ch 1, work sc2tog over first 2 sc, work sc2tog over last 2 sc, turn. *2 sc.*
Fasten off.

LONG WATER SPOUT Ⓓ

Using size C-2 (2.5mm) hook and B, ch 20.
Row 1 1 sl st in 2nd ch from hook, 1 sc in next ch, 1 hdc in next ch, 1 dc in each of next 10 ch, 1 hdc in next ch, 1 sc in next ch, join with a sl st to side of first sl st of row to form a loop, then work 1 sl st in each of last 4 ch.
Fasten off.

SHORT WATER SPOUT Ⓔ (make 2)

Using size C-2 (2.5mm) hook and B, ch 16.
Row 1 1 sl st in 2nd ch from hook, 1 sc in next ch, 1 hdc in next ch, 1 dc in each of next 6 ch, 1 hdc in next ch, 1 sc in next ch, join with a sl st to side of first sl st of row to form a loop, then work 1 sl st in each of last 4 ch.
Fasten off.

TO FINISH

Press pieces lightly on wrong side, following instructions on yarn label.

Bullion knot embroidery

Using a blunt-ended yarn needle, work five lines of bullion knots on both the right and left sides of the whale's body. Work each knot over one sc and work them one sc apart. Position the lines as follows:
Using B, work five bullion knots between 17th and 18th rows from foundation chain, working from right to left and working first knot over 13th sc from right side-edge.
Using B, work second line of bullion knots six rows above first line of knots. Begin second line of knots over 5th sc from right side-edge and work a total of 12 knots.
Work third and fourth lines of bullion knots in same way as second, each six rows above previous line of knots.
Work five bullion knots on fifth and final line of bullion knots as for first row and six rows above previous line
of knots.

Cross-stitch embroidery

Using a blunt-ended yarn needle, work four lines of cross-stitches (each over a long straight stitch) on both right and left sides of whale's body as follows:
Using B, work a long straight stitch between first two lines of bullion knots, working the stitch over 27 stitches and between 3rd and 4th rows (of the six rows between the lines of knots). Then using C, skip the first sc the straight stitch is worked over and work a cross-stitch over the next sc and over two rows so that the straight stitch is at center of cross-stitch. Work 12 more cross-stitches in the same way, each one sc apart.
In the remaining spaces between rows of bullion knots, work three more lines of cross-stitches in the same way as the first.

Whale seams

With wrong sides together, sew together tail sections of sides of body and fill tail firmly with washable stuffing.
Sew underbelly to sides of body, between foundation rows and 52nd rows. Sew remainder of seam to tail. Sew seam along top of whale, catching in ends of water spouts into seam as shown (see page 43).
Fill body firmly with washable stuffing, then sew foundation-row edges together at front of whale.

Eyes

For eyes, sew one small button to each side of body as shown.

Mouth

Using C for Blue Whale or B for Turquoise Whale, embroider mouth in backstitch as shown.

BEST BEACH BAG

This lovely little bag is made in no time at all. It is essential for carrying all those odds and ends that you will need or find when you take a trip to the beach. If you are worried that all your treasures might slip through the holes, you could stitch a simple lining into it.

BEFORE YOU BEGIN

SIZE
The finished bag measures approximately 6in/15cm wide by 6½in/16cm deep.

YARN
Rowan *4-Ply Cotton* (1¾oz/50g balls) as follows:

A	pale green (Fresh 131)	1 ball
B	turquoise (Aegean 129)	1 ball
C	navy (Navy 150)	1 ball

Rowan *Cotton Glace* (1¾oz/50g balls) as follows:

D	red (Poppy 741)	1 ball

HOOK
Size C-2 (2.5mm) crochet hook

GAUGE
One motif measures 2in/5cm square using size C-2 (2.5mm) crochet hook *or size necessary to obtain correct gauge.*

ABBREVIATIONS
See page 110.

GETTING STARTED

MOTIFS (make 18)
Using size C-2 (2.5mm) hook and A, ch 6 and join with a sl st to first ch to form a ring.
Round 1 (RS) Ch 3 (to count as first dc), 15 dc in ring, join with a sl st to 3rd of 3-ch. *16 sts.*
Fasten off.
(Do not turn at end of rounds, but work with RS always facing.)
Round 2 Join D with a sl st to any dc, ch 1, 1 sc in same place as sl st, *ch 3, skip next dc, 1 sc in next dc; rep from * 6 times more, ch 3, join with a sl st to first sc.
Fasten off.
Round 3 Join B with a sl st to any 3-ch sp, ch 3 (to count as first dc), [2 dc, ch 2, 3 dc] all in same 3-ch sp as sl st, *2 dc in next 3-ch sp, [3 dc, ch 2, 3 dc] all in next 3-ch sp; rep from * twice more, 2 dc in next 3-ch sp, join with a sl st to 3rd of 3-ch.
Fasten off.
Round 4 Join C with a sl st to any dc, ch 1, 1 sc in same place as sl st, then work 1 sc in each dc and 2 sc in each 2-ch sp (corner) to end of round, join with a sl st to first sc.
Fasten off.

EDGING PIECES (make 2)
Using size C-2 (2.5mm) hook and C, ch 33.
Foundation row 1 sc in 2nd ch from hook, 1 sc in each of rem ch, turn. *32 sc.*
Row 1 Ch 1 (does NOT count as a st), 1 sc in each sc to end, turn.
Row 2 Rep row 1.
Fasten off.

HANDLES (make 2)
Using size C-2 (2.5mm) hook and C, ch 43.
Foundation round (WS) 1 sc in 2nd ch from hook, 1 sc in each ch to last ch, 2 sc in last ch, then working along other side of foundation ch, skip first ch, 1 sc in each of next 41 ch, join with a sl st to first sc, turn. *84 sc.*
Round 1 Ch 1 (does NOT count as a st), 2 sc in first sc, 1 sc in each of next 40 sc, 2 sc in each of next 2 sc, 1 sc in each of next 40 sc, 2 sc in last sc, join with a sl st to first sc. *88 sc.*
Fasten off.

TO FINISH
Press pieces lightly on wrong side, following instructions on yarn label.
To make front of bag, join nine motifs together to form a square three motifs wide by three motifs deep. To do this, hold motifs together and work a sc through each pair of adjacent stitches,

leaving the 2 sc at each corner of each
motif free.
Make back of bag in same way with remaining
nine motifs.
Holding top of front of bag and last row of one
edging piece together, join them as follows:
Skip first sc on edging and
2 corner sc on first motif square,
then *[work 1 sc in next sc on both
layers] 8 times, skip next 3 sc on
edging and 2 corner sc of next
motif; rep from * once more,
[work 1 sc in next sc on both layers]
8 times.
Fasten off.
Join back of bag to remaining edging
piece in same way.
Join front to back in same way.
Fold each handle in half
lengthwise and sew together
along side edge.
Sew one handle to top of edging
on front of bag, with each end
1in/2.5cm from side seam. Sew
remaining handle to back of bag
in same way.

DOLORES DRESS

Dolores likes wearing this dress for special occasions because it is so simple and classic. Dainty edgings, pretty buttons, sweet pockets, and a lovely belt make it very special, indeed. Wear it with the Dolores Slippers (see page 58) for the perfect party outfit.

(see page 58)

SIZES AND MEASUREMENTS

To fit ages (in years)	2–3	3–4	4–5
To fit chest	22in	24in	26in
	56cm	61cm	66cm
Finished measurements			
Around chest	26in	28¾in	31in
	66cm	73cm	79cm
Length to shoulder	19¾in	22in	25¼in
	50cm	56cm	64cm

YARN

Rowan 4-Ply Soft (1¾oz/50g balls) as follows:

A	sage green (Leafy 367)	7 balls	7 balls	8 balls
B	red (Honk 374)	1 ball	1 ball	1 ball
C	pink (Fairy 395)	1 ball	1 ball	1 ball
D	pale blue (Whisper 370)	1 ball	1 ball	1 ball

HOOK

Size C-2 (2.5mm) crochet hook

EXTRAS

4 yellow buttons ⅝in/15mm in diameter

GAUGE

25 sts and 18 rows to 4in/10cm measured over main patt using size C-2 (2.5mm) crochet hook or size necessary to obtain correct gauge.
25 sts and 26 rows to 4in/10cm measured over sc using size C-2 (2.5mm) crochet hook or size necessary to obtain correct gauge.

ABBREVIATIONS

sc2tog = [insert hook in next st, yo and draw a loop through] twice, yo and draw through all 3 loops on hook—one st decreased.

dc2tog = [yo and insert hook in next st, yo and draw a loop through, yo and draw a loop through 2 loops on hook] twice, yo and draw through all 3 loops on hook—one st decreased. See also page 110.

See also page 110.

BACK

Using size C-2 (2.5mm) hook and A, ch 111 (123: 135).

Foundation row (RS) 1 hdc in 5th ch from hook, *ch 1, skip 1 ch, 1 hdc in next ch; rep from * to end, turn. *109 (121: 133) sts.*

Row 1 Ch 1 (does NOT count as a st), 1 sc in first hdc, *1 sc in next ch sp, 1 sc in next hdc; rep from * to end, 1 sc in next ch sp, 1 sc in 3rd of 4-ch, turn. *109 (121: 133) sc.*

Row 2 Ch 3 (to count as first hdc and first ch sp), skip first 2 sc, 1 hdc in next sc, *ch 1, skip 1 sc, 1 hdc in next sc; rep from * to end.

Row 3 Ch 1, 1 sc in first hdc, *1 sc in next ch sp, 1 sc in next hdc; rep from * to end, 1 sc in next ch sp, 1 sc in 2nd of 3-ch, turn.

Beg main patt as follows:

Main patt row 1 (RS) Ch 3 (to count as first dc), skip first sc, 1 dc in each sc to end, turn.

Main patt row 2 Ch 1 (does NOT count as a st), 1 sc in each dc to end, 1 sc in 3rd of 3-ch, turn.

(Last 2 rows form main patt when repeated.)

Next row (dec row) (RS) Ch 3, skip first sc, 1 dc in each of next 6 sc, work dc2tog over next 2 sc, 1 dc in each sc to last 9 sc, work dc2tog over next 2 sc, 1 dc in each of next 7 sc, turn.

Work even in main patt for 3 rows.

Rep last 4 rows 10 (12:14) times more and then the dec row again, ending with a RS row. *85 (93: 101) sts.*

Next row (WS) Ch 1, 1 sc in each dc to end, 1 sc in 3rd of 3-ch, turn.

Shape bodice

Next row (RS) Ch 1 (does NOT count as a st), 1 sc in each sc to end, turn.

(Last row forms simple sc patt when repeated.)
Working bodice in sc throughout, work even for 5 rows.

Next row (dec row) Ch 1, 1 sc in first sc, 1 sc in each of next 6 sc, work sc2tog over next 2 sc, 1 sc in each sc to last 9 sc, work sc2tog over next 2 sc, 1 sc in each of last 7 sc, turn. 83 (91: 99) sc.
Work even until Back measures 15 (17: 19¾) in/ 38 (43: 50) cm from beg, ending with a RS row.

Shape armholes

Next row (WS) 1 sl st in each of first 6 (7: 8) sc, ch 1, 1 sc in same place as last sl st, 1 sc in each sc to last 5 (6: 7) sc, turn. 73 (79: 85) sc.
Next row Ch 1, 1 sc in first sc, work sc2tog over next 2 sc, 1 sc in each sc to last 3 sc, work sc2tog over next 2 sc, 1 sc in last sc, turn.
Rep last row 4 times more. 63 (69: 75) sc.**
Work even until Back measures 19 (21¼: 24½) in/ 48 (54: 62) cm from beg, ending with a WS row.

Shape back neck

Next row (RS) Ch 1, 1 sc in first sc, 1 sc in each of next 15 (17: 19) sc, turn.
Work even for 4 rows.
Fasten off.
With RS facing, return to sts left unworked, skip center 31 (33: 35) sc and rejoin A with a sl st to next sc, ch 1, 1 sc in same place as sl st, 1 sc in each sc to end, turn.
Work even for 4 rows.
Fasten off.

FRONT

Work as for Back to **.
Work even until Front measures 17¼ (19¾: 22¾) in/44 (50: 58) cm from beg, ending with a WS row.

Shape front neck

Next row (RS) Ch 1, 1 sc in first sc, 1 sc in each of next 15 (17: 19) sc, turn.
Work even until Front measures same as Back to shoulder.
Fasten off.
With RS facing, return to sts left unworked, skip center 31 (33: 35) sc and rejoin A with a sl st to next sc, ch 1, 1 sc in same place as sl st, 1 sc in each sc to end, turn.

Work even until Front measures same as Back to shoulder.
Fasten off.

SLEEVES (make 2)

Using size C-2 (2.5mm) hook and A, ch 67 (73: 79).
Foundation row (RS) 1 hdc in 5th ch from hook, *ch 1, skip 1 ch, 1 hdc in next ch; rep from * to end, turn. 65 (71: 77) sts.
Row 1 Ch 1 (does NOT count as a st), 1 sc in first hdc, *1 sc in next ch sp, 1 sc in next hdc; rep from * to end, 1 sc in next ch sp, 1 sc in 3rd of 4-ch, turn. 65 (71: 77) sc.
Row 2 Ch 3 (to count as first hdc and first ch sp), skip first 2 sc, 1 hdc in next sc, *ch 1, skip 1 sc, 1 hdc in next sc; rep from * to end.
Row 3 Ch 1, 1 sc in first hdc, *1 sc in next ch sp, 1 sc in next hdc; rep from * to end, 1 sc in next ch sp, 1 sc in 2nd of 3-ch, turn.
Row 4 Ch 1, 1 sc in each sc to end, turn.
(Last row forms simple sc patt when repeated.)
Cont in sc throughout, beg sleeve shaping as follows:
Next row (inc row) Ch 1, 1 sc in each of first 3 sc, 2 sc in next sc, 1 sc in each sc to last 4 sc, 2 sc in next sc, 1 sc in each of last 3 sc, turn.
Work even for 2 rows.
Rep last 3 rows 0 (1: 2) times more.
Next row (inc row) Ch 1, 1 sc in each of first 3 sc, 2 sc in next sc, 1 sc in each sc to last 4 sc, 2 sc in next sc, 1 sc in each of last 3 sc, turn. 69 (77: 85) sc.
Work even for 3 (2: 1) rows.

Shape top of sleeve

Next row 1 sl st in each of first 6 (7: 8) sc, ch 1, 1 sc in same place as last sl st, 1 sc in each sc to last 5 (6: 7) sc, turn. 59 (65: 71) sc.
Next row Ch 1, 1 sc in first sc, work sc2tog over next 2 sc, 1 sc in each sc to last 3 sc, work sc2tog over next 2 sc, 1 sc in last sc, turn.
Rep last row 4 times more. 49 (55: 61) sc.
Fasten off.

POCKETS (make 2)

Using size C-2 (2.5mm) hook and A, ch 20.
Foundation row (RS) 1 sc in 2nd ch from hook, 1 sc in each of rem ch, turn. 19 sc.

Row 1 (patt row) Ch 1, 1 sc in each sc to end, turn.

(Last row forms simple sc patt when repeated.)

Row 2 (inc row) Ch 1, 1 sc in each of first 3 sc, *2 sc in next sc, 1 sc in each of next 2 sc; rep from * 3 times more, 2 sc in next sc, 1 sc in each of last 3 sc, turn. 24 sc.

Cont in sc throughout, work even for 5 rows, ending with a WS row.

Next row (inc row) (RS) Ch 1, 1 sc in each of first 2 sc, *2 sc in next sc, 1 sc in each of next 2 sc; rep from * 5 times more, 2 sc in next sc, 1 sc in each of last 3 sc, turn. 31 sc.

Work even for 5 rows, ending with a WS row.

Next row (dec row) (RS) Ch 1, 1 sc in each of first 2 sc, *work sc2tog over next 2 sc, 1 sc in each of next 2 sc; rep from * 5 times more, work sc2tog over next 2 sc, 1 sc in each of last 3 sc. 24 sc.

Fasten off.

Edging

With RS facing for each of the 4 rows of the pocket edging, join on a new color on each row as follows:

Next row (RS) Join D with a sl st to first sc, ch 1, 1 sc in same sc as sl st, 1 sc in each sc to end.

Fasten off.

Rep last row 3 times more, working one row each in A, C, and B.

BELT

Using size C-2 (2.5mm) hook and B, ch 220 (240: 260).

Foundation row (RS) 1 sc in 2nd ch from hook, 1 sc in each of rem ch.

Fasten off.

With RS facing for each of rem 6 rows of belt, join on a new color on each row as follows:

Row 1 (RS) Join C with a sl st to first sc, ch 1 (does NOT count as a st), 1 sc in same sc as sl st, 1 sc in each sc to end.

Fasten off.

Row 2 (RS) Using A, rep row 1.

Fasten off.

Row 3 (buttonhole row) (RS) Join D with a sl st to first sc, ch 1, 1 sc in same sc as sl st, ch 3, skip next 3 sc, 1 sc in each of next 18 sc, ch 3, skip next 3 sc, 1 sc in each sc to end.

Fasten off.

Row 4 (RS) Join A with a sl st to first sc, ch 1, 1 sc in same sc as sl st, then work 1 sc in each sc and 3 sc in each 3-ch sp to end.

Fasten off.

Row 5 (RS) Using C, rep row 1.

Fasten off.

Work final row of belt along row-end edges (short side edges) of belt and along top of previous row as follows:

Row 6 (RS) Join B with a sl st to end of foundation row at right end of belt, ch 1, 1 sc in same place as sl st, 1 sc in each row-end to corner, 2 sc in first sc of previous row, 1 sc in each sc to last sc, 2 sc in last sc, 1 sc in each row-end along this end of belt.

Fasten off.

BELT LOOPS (make 3)

Using size C-2 (2.5mm) hook and A, ch 7.

Foundation row (RS) 1 sc in 2nd ch from hook, 1 sc in each of rem ch, turn. 6 sc.

Row 1 Ch 1 (does NOT count as a st), 1 sc in each sc to end.

Fasten off.

TO FINISH

Press pieces lightly on wrong side, following instructions on yarn label.

Sew shoulder seams.

Sew sleeves to armholes. Sew side and sleeve seams.

Lower edging

With RS facing and using size C-2 (2.5mm) hook and C, work edging along foundation-chain edges of Front and Back as follows:

Round 1 (RS) Join C with a sl st to foundation-chain edge of Front at right side seam, ch 1, 1 sc in same place as sl st, 1 sc in each foundation ch to end, join with a sl st to first sc.

Fasten off.

(Do not turn at end of round, but cont with RS facing.)

Round 2 Join B with a sl st to first sc, *ch 5, 1 sl st in first ch, 1 sc in each of next 3 sc; rep from * to end, join with a sl st to first ch. Fasten off.

Sleeve edging
With RS facing and using size C-2 (2.5mm) hook, join C to foundation-chain edge of Sleeve at sleeve seam and work edging as for lower edging.

Sew pockets to front of dress as shown right, stitching them in place with side edges parallel so that top of pocket puffs outward.
Sew one belt loop to each side seam and one to the center of the back. Thread belt through loops.
Sew two buttons to belt to fit.
Sew two buttons below neck for decoration as shown right.

DOLORES SLIPPERS

You will never want to take these dainty little Dolores Slippers off as they are comfortable and very practical. They really will keep your feet warm on chilly fall days. Dress them up with the sweetest button you can find—lovely!

BEFORE YOU BEGIN

SIZES AND MEASUREMENTS

To fit ages (in years)	2–3	3–4	4–5
Length of slippers	5¾ in	6¼ in	6¾ in
	14.5cm	16cm	17.5cm

YARN

Rowan *4-Ply Soft* (1¾ oz/50g balls) as follows:

A sea green (Folly 391)   1 ball 1 ball 1 ball
B charcoal (Sooty 372)   1 ball 1 ball 1 ball

Small amount of each of the following colors:

C red (Honk 374)
D pink (Fairy 395)
E sage green (Leafy 391)
F pale blue (Whisper 370)

HOOK

Size C-2 (2.5mm) crochet hook

EXTRAS

2 small buttons

GAUGE

25 sts and 26 rows to 4in/10cm measured over sc using size C-2 (2.5mm) crochet hook *or size necessary to obtain correct gauge.*

ABBREVIATIONS

See page 110.

GETTING STARTED

SLIPPERS (make 2)

Using size C-2 (2.5mm) hook and A, ch 21.

Sole

Foundation round (WS) 1 sc in 2nd ch from hook, 1 sc in each ch to last ch, 3 sc in last ch, then working along other side of foundation ch, skip first ch, 1 sc in each of last 19 ch, join with a sl st to first ch, turn. *41 sc.*

(**Note:** When working the rounds, the work is turned at the heel-end of the sole. Remember to turn at end of each round.)

Round 1 (RS) Ch 1 (does NOT count as a st), 2 sc in first sc, 1 sc in each of next 18 sc, 2 sc in each of next 3 sc, 1 sc in each of next 18 sc, 2 sc in last sc, join with a sl st to 1-ch, turn. 46 sc.

Round 2 Ch 1, 2 sc in first sc, 1 sc in each of next 20 sc, 2 sc in each of next 4 sc, 1 sc in each of next 20 sc, 2 sc in last sc, join with a sl st to 1-ch, turn. 52 sc.

Do not cut off yarn, but leave a long loop to return to.

With RS facing, join in a spare length of A on next row and work 2 extra rows of shaping at toe-end of sole as follows:

Next row (RS) Using a spare length of A, skip first 17 sc and join on yarn with a sl st to next sc, ch 1, 1 sl st in same place as first sl st, 1 sc in each of next 7 sc, 2 sc in each of next 2 sc, 1 sc in each of next 7 sc, 1 sl st in next sc, turn.

Next row 1 sl st in next sc, 1 sc in each of next 7 sc, 2 sc in each of next 2 sc, 1 sc in each of next 7 sc, 1 sl st in next sc, turn. 56 *sts all around sole.*

Cut off spare length of A.

Return to main ball of A and work next round as follows:

Round 3 (RS) Ch 1, 2 sc in first sc, 1 sc in each of next 26 sts, 2 sc in each of next 2 sc, 1 sc in each of next 26 sts, 2 sc in last sc, join with a sl st to 1-ch, turn. 60 *sc.*

Do not cut off yarn, but leave a long loop to return to.

Again work 2 extra rows of shaping at toe-end of sole as follows:

Next row (WS) Using a spare length of A, skip first 13 sc and join on yarn with a sl st to next sc, ch 1, 1 sl st in same place as first sl st, 1 sc in each of next 15 sc, 2 sc in each of next 2 sc, 1 sc in each of next 15 sc, 1 sl st in next sc, turn.

Next row 1 sl st in next sc, 1 sc in each of next 15 sc, 2 sc in each of next 2 sc, 1 sc in each of next 15 sc, 1 sl st in next sc, turn. *64 sts all around sole.*

Cut off spare length of A.

Return to main ball of A and work next round as follows:

Round 4 (WS) Ch 1, 2 sc in first sc, 1 sc in each of next 30 sts, 2 sc in each of next 2 sc, 1 sc in each of next 30 sts, 2 sc in last sc, join with a sl st to 1-ch, turn. *68 sc.*

Do not cut off yarn, but leave a long loop to return to.

Again work 2 extra rows of shaping at toe-end of sole as follows:

Next row (RS) Using a spare length of A, skip first 9 sc and join on yarn with a sl st to next sc, ch 1, 1 sl st in same place as first sl st, 1 sc in each of next 23 sc, 2 sc in each of next 2 sc, 1 sc in each of next 23 sc, 1 sl st in next sc, turn.

Next row 1 sl st in next sc, 1 sc in each of next 23 sc, 2 sc in each of next 2 sc, 1 sc in each of next 23 sc, 1 sl st in next sc, turn. *72 sts all around sole.*

Cut off spare length of A.

Return to main ball of A complete sole in rounds as follows:

Round 5 (RS) Ch 1, 2 sc in first sc, 1 sc in each of next 32 sts, 2 sc in next sc, 1 sc in each of next 4 sc, 2 sc in next sc, 1 sc in each of next 32 sts, 2 sc in last sc, join with a sl st to 1-ch, turn. *76 sc.*

Round 6 Ch 1, 2 sc in first sc, 1 sc in each of next 33 sc, 2 sc in next sc, 1 sc in each of next 6 sc, 2 sc in next sc, 1 sc in each of next 33 sc, 2 sc in last sc, join with a sl st to 1-ch, turn. *80 sc.*

Work 2 (4: 6) rounds more in this way (as set by rounds 5 and 6), working each round with 1 sc more between increases along each side edge of sole and 2 sc more between increases at toe-end of sole, ending with a WS row. *88 (96: 104) sc.*

Cut off A.

Upper section of slipper
Change to B and cont as follows:

Next round Using B, ch 1, 1 sc in each sc, join with a sl st to 1-ch, turn.

Rep last round 4 (6: 8) times more, ending with a RS row.

Do not cut off yarn, but leave a long loop to return to.

With WS facing, join in a spare length of B on next row and work 6 extra rows of shaping at toe-end of slipper as follows:

Next row (WS) Using a spare length of B, skip first 20 (22: 24) sc and join on yarn with a sl st to next sc, ch 1, 1 sl st in same place as first sl st, 1 sc in each of next 22 (24: 26) sc, skip next 2 sc, 1 sc in each of next 22 (24: 26) sc, 1 sl st in next sc, turn.

Next row 1 sl st in next sc, 1 sc in each of next 20 (22: 24) sc, skip next 2 sc, 1 sc in each of next 20 (22: 24) sc, 1 sl st in next sc, turn.

Next row 1 sl st in next sc, 1 sc in each of next 18 (20: 22) sc, skip next 2 sc, 1 sc in each of next 18 (20: 22) sc, 1 sl st in next sc, turn.

Next row 1 sl st in next sc, 1 sc in each of next 16 (18: 20) sc, skip next 2 sc, 1 sc in each of next 16 (18: 20) sc, 1 sl st in next sc, turn.

Next row 1 sl st in next sc, 1 sc in each of next 14 (16: 18) sc, skip next 2 sc, 1 sc in each of next 14 (16: 18) sc, 1 sl st in next sc, turn.

Next row 1 sl st in next sc, 1 sc in each of next 12 (14: 16) sc, skip next 2 sc, 1 sc in each of next 12 (14: 16) sc, 1 sl st in next sc, turn. *76 (84: 92) sts.*

Cut off spare length of B.

Return to main ball of B and work next round as follows:

Next round (WS) Ch 1, 1 sc in each of next 20 (22: 24) sc, 1 sc in each of next 6 sl sts, 1 sc in each of next 11 (13: 15) sc, skip next 2 sc, 1 sc in each of next 11 (13: 15) sc, 1 sc in each of next 6 sl sts, 1 sc in each of next 20 (22: 24) sc, join with a sl st to 1-ch, turn.

Cut off B.

With RS always facing, cont in stripes as follows:

Next round (RS) Using C, ch 1, 1 sc in each of first 36 (40: 44) sc, skip next 2 sc, 1 sc in each of next 36 (40: 44) sc, join with a sl st to 1-ch, do not turn.

Cut off C.

Next round (RS) Using D, ch 1, 1 sc in each of first 35 (39: 43) sc, skip next 2 sc, 1 sc in each of next 35 (39: 43) sc, join with a sl st to 1-ch, do not turn.

Cut off D.

Next round Using E, ch 1, 1 sc in each of first 34 (38: 42) sc, skip next 2 sc, 1 sc in each of next 34 (38: 42) sc, join with a sl st to 1-ch, do not turn. Cut off E.

Next round Using F, ch 1, 1 sc in each of first 33 (37: 41) sc, skip next 2 sc, 1 sc in each of next 33 (37: 41) sc, join with a sl st to 1-ch, do not turn. Fasten off.

With RS still facing, change to D and work two rows as follows:

Next row (RS) Skip first 26 (28: 30) sc, join D with a sl st to next sc, ch 1, 1 sl st in same place as first sl st, 1 sc in each of next 5 (7: 9) sc, skip next 2 sc, 1 sc in each of next 5 (7: 9) sc, 1 sl st in nex⁻ sc, turn.

Next row (WS) Using D, 1 sl st in next sc, 1 sc in each of next 3 (5: 7) sc, skip next 2 sc, 1 sc in each of next 3 (5: 7) sc, 1 sl st in next sc. Fasten off.

With RS facing, return to beg of round and join C with a sl st to first sc, ch 1, 1 sc in same place as sl st, then work in sc to end of round decreasing at toe as before, join with a sl st to 1-ch. Fasten off.

STRAPS (make 2)

Using size C-2 (2.5mm) hook and C, ch 41 (45: 49).

Foundation round (RS) 1 sc in 7th ch from hook, 1 sc in each ch to last ch, 3 sc in last ch, then working along other side of foundation ch, skip first ch, 1 sc in each ch to last 6 ch (that form buttonhole loop), join with a sl st to first sc. Fasten off.

TO FINISH

Sew center 16 sc of one strap to center of back of each slipper.

Sew a button to end of strap on each slipper to correspond with buttonhole loop.

ARIADNE DOLL

Ariadne enjoys walking in the park with her little dog Hercule. They often go shopping together. Ariadne likes to buy flowers for herself and treats for Hercule.

BEFORE YOU BEGIN

SIZE
The finished doll measures approximately 13½in/34cm tall, including hat.

YARN
Rowan *4-Ply Soft* (1¾oz/50g balls) as follows:

Doll with red skirt

A red (Honk 374)		1 ball
B sea green (Folly 391)		1 ball
C sage green (Leafy 367)		1 ball
D charcoal (Sooty 372)		1 ball
E ecru (Linseed 393)		1 ball
F pink (Fairy 395)		small amount

Doll with pink skirt

A pink (Fairy 395)		1 ball
B red (Honk 374)		1 ball
C sea green (Folly 391)		1 ball
D charcoal (Sooty 372)		1 ball
E ecru (Linseed 393)		1 ball

HOOKS
Size C-2 (2.5mm) crochet hook
Size B-1 (2mm) crochet hook

EXTRAS
1 button ⁷⁄₁₆in/11mm in diameter, to decorate belt

GAUGE
25 sts and 26 rows to 4in/10cm measured over sc using size C-2 (2.5mm) crochet hook *or size necessary to obtain correct gauge.*

ABBREVIATIONS
sc2tog = [insert hook in next st, yo and draw a loop through] twice, yo and draw through all 3 loops on hook—*one st decreased.*
See also page 110.

DOLL WITH RED SKIRT
FRONT OF DOLL Ⓐ
The front and the back of the doll are each worked in one piece from the hem of the skirt to the top of the head. (The arms and legs are worked separately and stitched on later.)

Skirt
Using size C-2 (2.5mm) hook and A, ch 29.
Foundation row (RS) 1 sc in 2nd ch from hook, 1 sc in each of rem ch, turn. *28 sc.*
Row 1 Ch 1 (does NOT count as a st), 1 sc in each sc to end, turn.
Rows 2 and 3 [Rep row 1] twice.
To help keep track of which is RS of piece, after turning work and before beg next row, mark this side of work as RS with a colored thread.
Row 4 (dec row) (RS) Ch 1, work sc2tog over first 2 sc, 1 sc in each sc to last 2 sc, work sc2tog over last 2 sc, turn.
Rows 5–8 [Rep row 1] 4 times.
Rows 9–23 [Rep rows 4–8] 3 times. *20 sc.*
Row 24 Rep row 4. *18 sc.*
Rows 25–27 [Rep row 1] 3 times.
Cut off A.
This completes the skirt front.

Belt
Change to D and work doll's belt as follows:
Rows 28 and 29 [Rep row 1] twice.
Cut off D.

Sweater
Change to B and work front of doll's sweater as follows:
Rows 30–36 [Rep row 1] 7 times.
Row 37 Rep row 4. *16 sc.*
Rows 38–43 [Rep row 1] 6 times.
Row 44 Rep row 4.
Row 45 Rep row 1.
Rows 46–53 [Rep rows 44 and 45] 4 times. *6 sc.*
Cut off B.

Head

Change to E and work head as follows:

Row 54 Rep row 4. *4 sc.*

Row 55 Rep row 1.

Row 56 Ch 1, 2 sc in first sc, 1 sc in each sc to last sc, 2 sc in last sc. *6 sc.*

Rows 57–59 [Rep row 56] 3 times. *12 sc.***

Rows 60 and 61 [Rep row 1] twice.

Nose and top of head

Row 62 (RS) Ch 1, 1 sc in each of first 6 sc, ch 5 (for nose), 1 sl st in base of last sc, 1 sc in each of next 6 sc, turn.

Keeping nose on RS of work, complete head as follows:

Rows 63 and 64 [Rep row 1] twice.

Row 65 Rep row 4. *10 sc.*

Row 66 Rep row 1.

Rows 67–70 [Rep row 4] 4 times. *2 sc.*

Fasten off.

BACK OF DOLL Ⓑ

Work as for front of doll to **.

Top of head

Rows 60–64 [Rep row 1] 5 times.

Row 65 Rep row 4. *10 sc.*

Row 66 Rep row 1.

Rows 67–70 [Rep row 4] 4 times. *2 sc.*

Fasten off.

LEGS Ⓒ (make 2)

Each leg is worked in one piece from the shoe to the top of the leg.

Shoe section

Using size C-2 (2.5mm) hook and C, ch 7 and join with a sl st to first ch to form a ring.

Round 1 (RS) Ch 1, 6 sc in ring.

(**Note:** The legs are worked in a spiral with RS always facing; so to keep track of where each round begins and ends, place a marker at end of each round.)

Round 2 1 sc in each sc to end of round.

Rounds 3–6 [Rep round 2] 4 times.

Cut off C.

Leg section

Change to E and rep round 2 until leg measures 4in/10cm from beg (including shoe section).

Fasten off.

ARMS Ⓓ (make 2)

Each arm is worked in one piece from the hand to the top of the sleeve.

Hand section

Using size C-2 (2.5mm) hook and E, ch 7 and join with a sl st to first ch to form a ring.

Round 1 (RS) Ch 1, 6 sc in ring.

(**Note:** The arms are worked in a spiral with RS

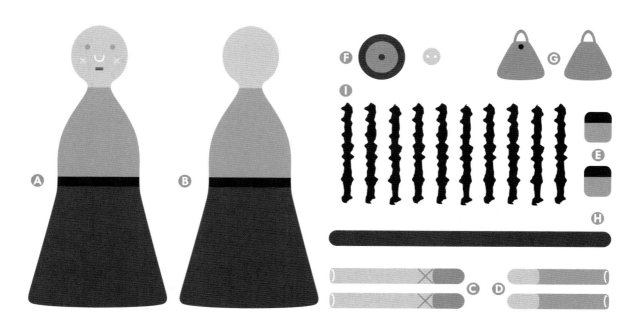

always facing until top of sleeve is reached; so to keep track of where each round begins and ends, place a marker at end of each round.)
Round 2 1 sc in each sc to end of round.
Rounds 3–7 [Rep round 2] 5 times.
Cut off E.

Sleeve
Change to B and work sleeve as follows:
Rounds 8–15 [Rep round 2] 8 times.
Round 16 1 sc in each sc to end of round, *turn*.

Shape top of sleeve
Work top of sleeve back and forth in rows as follows:
Next row (WS) Ch 1 (does NOT count as a st), 1 sc in each of first 3 sc, turn.
Next row Ch 1, 1 sc in each of 3 sc, turn.
Rep last row once more.
Fasten off, leaving a long tail-end of yarn for sewing arm to body.

POCKETS E (make 2)
Using size C-2 (2.5mm) hook and B, ch 5.
Foundation row (RS) 1 sc in 2nd ch from hook, 1 sc in each of rem ch, turn. 4 sc.
Row 1 Ch 1 (does NOT count as a st), 1 sc in each sc to end, turn.
Rows 2 and 3 [Rep row 1] twice.
Cut off B.

Pocket top edging
Change to D and work edging as follows:
Rows 4 and 5 [Rep row 1] twice.
Fasten off.

HAT F
Using size C-2 (2.5mm) hook and C, ch 6 and join with a sl st to first ch to form a ring.
Round 1 (RS) Ch 1, 5 sc in ring.
(Note: The hat is worked in a spiral with RS always facing; so to keep track of where each round begins and ends, place a marker at end of each round.)
Round 2 2 sc in each sc to end of round. *10 sc*.
Round 3 Rep round 2. *20 sc*.
Round 4 1 sc in each sc to end of round.
Round 5 Rep round 4.
Cut off C.

Hat edging
Change to A and work hat edging as follows:
Round 6 *1 sc in next sc, 2 sc in next sc; rep from * 9 times more.
Fasten off.

BAG PIECES G (make 2)
Using size C-2 (2.5mm) hook and C, ch 8.
Foundation row (RS) 1sc in 2nd ch from hook, 1 sc in each of rem ch, turn. 7 sc.
Row 1 Ch 1 (does NOT count as a st), 1 sc in each sc to end, turn.
Row 2 Rep row 1.
Row 3 Ch 1, work sc2tog over first 2 sc, 1 sc in each sc to last 2 sc, work sc2tog over last 2 sc, turn. 5 sc.
Rows 4 and 5 [Rep row 1] twice.
Row 6 Rep row 3. 3 sc.
Row 7 Rep row 1.

Handle
Row 8 Ch 10, skip first 2 sc, 1 sl st in last sc.
Fasten off.

SCARF H
Using size C-2 (2.5mm) hook and A, ch 60.
Round 1 (RS) 1 sc in 2nd ch from hook, 1 sc in each ch to last ch, 2 sc in last ch, then working along other side of foundation ch, skip first ch, 1 sc in each ch to last ch, 1 sl st in last ch.
Fasten off.

HAIR STRANDS I (make 10)
Using size B-1 (2mm) hook and D, ch 50 and fasten off.

TO FINISH
Do not press.

Face
Using a blunt-ended yarn needle for all embroidery, work face embroidery as follows:
For mouth, use A to work three straight stitches 2 sc wide on top of each other, positioning them two rows below nose.
For each eye, use B to work one bullion knot one row above nose and 2 sc from center sc.
For each cheek, use F to work a small cross-stitch two rows below eye.

Pockets and belt

Sew pockets to front of skirt three rows below belt and 5 sc apart.

Sew button to center of belt on front of doll.

Body

Leaving last three rows at top of sweater open and hem-edge of skirt open, sew back of body to front of body.

Sew top of each sleeve to opening in seam at top of sweater.

Fill body firmly with washable stuffing.

Pin legs to center of skirt hem and 3 sc apart so that about 1¼in/3cm of top of each leg will be inside of skirt; then sew together skirt-hem edges, catching in legs.

Shoe ribbons

Using C, embroider a large cross-stitch above each shoe on front of doll, then a straight stitch across back of leg at top of cross-stitch to imitate shoe ribbons.

Hair

Twist ends of each hair strand in opposite directions so that length of chain curls.

Sew center of each of 10 strands of hair to top of head.

Hat tassel

Using size C-2 (2.5mm) hook and A, ch 6 and fasten off.

Sew tassel just made to top of hat, using one tail-end of yarn, then weave other tail-end into tassel.

Sew hat to top of doll's head, covering hair seam.

Scarf

Wrap scarf around doll's neck and sew in place.

Bag

Using D, make a bullion knot on right side at center of last row on one bag piece.

Sew bag pieces together.

Sew bag handles to one of doll's hands.

ANNIE V-NECK VEST

Annie thinks this little V-neck vest with its lovely textured stitch is just the thing to wear on an fall day. Find a favorite button for it like Annie's, to make it look extra special.

BEFORE YOU BEGIN

SIZES AND MEASUREMENTS

To fit ages (in years)	2–3	3–4	4–5
To fit chest	22in	24in	26in
	56cm	61cm	66cm
Finished measurements			
Around chest	26in	28in	30in
	66cm	71cm	76cm
Length to shoulder	11½in	12¾in	13¾in
	29cm	32cm	35cm

YARN

Rowan *Pure Wool DK* (1¾oz/50g balls) as follows:

gold (Honey 033)	4 balls	4 balls	5 balls

HOOKS

Size D-3 (3mm) crochet hook
Size E-4 (3.5mm) crochet hook

EXTRAS

1 button ¾in/2cm in diameter

GAUGE

20 sts and 24 rows to 4in/10cm measured over sc using size E-4 (3.5mm) crochet hook *or size necessary to obtain correct gauge.*

ABBREVIATIONS

See page 110.

GETTING STARTED

BACK

Using size D-3 (3mm) hook, ch 62 (67: 72).
Foundation row (RS) Yo and insert hook in 3rd ch from hook, yo and draw a loop through ch and through first loop on hook, yo and draw through rem 2 loops on hook, *yo and insert hook in next ch, yo and draw a loop through ch and through first loop on hook, yo and draw through rem 2 loops on hook; rep from * to end, turn. 61 *(66: 71) sts.*
Row 1 (patt row) Ch 2 (to count as first st), skip first st, *yo and insert hook in next st, yo and draw a loop through st and through first loop on hook, yo and draw through rem 2 loops on hook; rep from * to end, working last st in 2nd of 2-ch, turn.
Rep last row 5 times more, ending with a RS row. Change to size E-4 (3.5mm) hook.**
Next row (WS) Ch 1 (does NOT count as a st), 1 sc in first st, *ch 2, skip next st, 1 sc in next st, ch 2, skip next 2 sts, 1 sc in next st; rep from * to end, working last sc in 2nd of 2-ch, turn.
Beg main patt as follows:
Main patt row 1 (RS) Ch 3 (to count as first dc), 1 dc in first sc, *3 dc in next sc; rep from * to last sc, 2 dc in last sc, turn. 23 *(25: 27) 3-dc groups.*
Main patt row 2 Ch 1 (does NOT count as a st), 1 sc in first dc, *ch 2, skip next 2 dc, 1 sc in next dc; rep from * to end, working last sc in 3rd of 3-ch, turn.
(Last 2 rows form main patt when repeated.)
Work 9 (11: 13) rows more in patt, ending with a RS row.

Shape sleeves

Next row (WS) Ch 1 (does NOT count as a st), 1 sc in first dc, [ch 2, skip 1 dc, 1 sc in next dc] 3 times, *ch 2, skip next 2 dc, 1 sc in next dc; rep from * to last 6 sts, [ch 2, skip 1 dc, 1 sc in next dc] 3 times, working last sc in 3rd of 3-ch, turn.
Next row Ch 3 (to count as first dc), 1dc in first sc, *3 dc in next sc; rep from * to last sc, 2 dc in last sc, turn. *(2 3-dc groups increased.)*
Rep last 2 rows twice more.
Mark each end of last row with a colored thread.
Work even in patt for 16 (18: 20) rows.
Fasten off.

FRONT

Work as given for Back to **.
Divide for front opening

Divide for front opening as follows:

1st and 3rd sizes only:
Next row (WS) Ch 1 (does NOT count as a st), 1 sc in first st, [ch 2, skip next st, 1 sc in next st, ch 2, skip next 2 sts, 1 sc in next st] 5 (—: 6) times, turn.

2nd size only:
Next row (WS) Ch 1 (does NOT count as a st), 1 sc in first st, [ch 2, skip next st, 1 sc in next st, ch 2, skip next 2 sts, 1 sc in next st] 5 times, ch 2, skip next st, 1 sc in next st, turn.

All sizes:
Working on these sts only for right front, beg main patt as follows:
Main patt row 1 (RS) Ch 3 (to count as first dc), 1 dc in first sc, *3 dc in next sc; rep from * to last sc, 2 dc in last sc, turn. 9 (10: 11) 3-dc groups.
Main patt row 2 Ch 1 (does NOT count as a st), 1 sc in first dc, *ch 2, skip next 2 dc, 1 sc in next dc; rep from * to end, working last sc in 3rd of 3-ch, turn.
(Last 2 rows form main patt when repeated.)
Work 6 (8: 10) rows more in patt, ending with a WS row.

Shape right front neck
Next row (dec row) (RS) Ch 3 (to count as first dc), 1 dc in first sc, 1 dc in next sc, 1 dc in next 2-ch sp, 1 dc in next sc, *3 dc in next sc; rep from * to last sc, 2 dc in last sc, turn. *(1 dc group decreased at neck edge.)*
Work even in patt for 2 rows, ending with a RS row.

Shape sleeve
Next row (WS) Ch 1 (does NOT count as a st), 1 sc in first dc, [ch 2, skip 1 dc, 1 sc in next dc] 3 times, *ch 2, skip next 2 dc, 1 sc in next dc; rep from * to end, working last sc in 3rd of 3-ch, turn.
Next row Ch 3 (to count as first dc), 1 dc in first sc, *3 dc in next sc; rep from * to last sc, 2 dc in last sc, turn. *(1 3-dc group increased.)*
Next row Ch 1 (does NOT count as a st), 1 sc in first dc, [ch 2, skip 1 dc, 1 sc in next dc] 3 times, *ch 2, skip next 2 dc, 1 sc in next dc; rep from * to end, working last sc in 3rd of 3-ch, turn.
Next row Ch 3 (to count as first dc), 1 dc in first sc, 1 dc in next sc, 1 dc in next 2-ch sp, 1 dc in

next sc, *3 dc in next sc; rep from * to last sc, 2 dc in last sc, turn. *(1 dc group decreased at neck edge.)*
Next row Ch 1 (does NOT count as a st), 1 sc in first dc, [ch 2, skip 1 dc, 1 sc in next dc] 3 times, *ch 2, skip next 2 dc, 1 sc in next dc; rep from * to end, working last sc in 3rd of 3-ch, turn.
Next row Ch 3 (to count as first dc), 1 dc in first sc, *3 dc in next sc; rep from * to last sc, 2 dc in last sc, turn.
Mark side-seam edge of last row with a colored thread.
Work even in patt for 3 rows, ending with a WS row.
Cont in patt, work neck decrease as set on next row and then on foll 6th row, ending with a RS row.
Work even in patt for 6 (8: 10) rows (Front should now match same length as Back to shoulder).
Fasten off.

1st and 3rd sizes only:
With WS facing, skip center 9 sts and rejoin yarn with a sl st to next st, 1 sc in same place as sl st, [ch 2, skip next st, 1 sc in next st, ch 2, skip next 2 sts, 1 sc in next st] 5 (—: 6) times, working last sc in 2nd of 2-ch, turn.

2nd size only:
With WS facing, skip center 9 sts and rejoin yarn with a sl st to next st, 1 sc in same place as sl st, ch 2, skip next 2 sts, 1 sc in next st, [ch 2, skip next st, 1 sc in next st, ch 2, skip next 2 sts, 1 sc in next st] 5 times, working last sc in 2nd of 2-ch, turn.

All sizes:
Beg main patt as follows:
Main patt row 1 (RS) Ch 3 (to count as first dc), 1 dc in first sc, *3 dc in next sc; rep from * to last sc, 2 dc in last sc, turn. 9 (10: 11) 3-dc groups.
Main patt row 2 Ch 1 (does not count as a st), 1 sc in first dc, *ch 2, skip next 2 dc, 1 sc in next dc; rep from * to end, working last sc in 3rd of 3-ch, turn.
(Last 2 rows form main patt when repeated.)

Work 6 (8: 10) rows more in patt, ending with a WS row.

Shape left front neck

Next row (dec row) (RS) Ch 3 (to count as first dc), 1 dc in first sc, *3 dc in next sc; rep from * to last 3 sc, 1 dc in next sc, 1 dc in next 2-ch sp, 1 dc in next sc, 2 dc in last sc, turn. *(1 dc group decreased at neck edge.)*
Work even in patt for 2 rows, ending with a RS row.

Shape sleeve

Next row (WS) Ch 1 (does NOT count as a st), 1 sc in first dc, *ch 2, skip next 2 dc, 1 sc in next dc; rep from * to last 6 sts, [ch 2, skip 1 dc, 1 sc in next dc] 3 times, working last sc in 3rd of 3-ch, turn.
Next row Ch 3 (to count as first dc), 1 dc in first sc, *3 dc in next sc; rep from * to last sc, 2 dc in last sc, turn. *(1 3-dc group increased.)*
Next row Ch 1 (does NOT count as a st), 1 sc in first dc, *ch 2, skip next 2 dc, 1 sc in next dc; rep from * to last 6 sts, [ch 2, skip 1 dc, 1 sc in next dc] 3 times, working last sc in 3rd of 3-ch, turn.
Next row Ch 3 (to count as first dc), 1 dc in first sc, *3 dc in next sc; rep from * to last 3 sc, 1 dc in next sc, 1 dc in next 2-ch sp, 1 dc in next sc, 2 dc in last sc, turn. *(1 dc group decreased at neck edge.)*
Next row Ch 1 (does NOT count as a st), 1 sc in first dc, *ch 2, skip next 2 dc, 1 sc in next dc; rep from * to last 6 sts, [ch 2, skip 1 dc, 1 sc in next dc] 3 times, working last sc in 3rd of 3-ch, turn.
Next row Ch 3 (to count as first dc), 1 dc in first sc, *3 dc in next sc; rep from * to last sc, 2 dc in last sc, turn.
Mark side-seam edge of last row with a colored thread.
Work even in patt for 3 rows, ending with a WS row.
Cont in patt, work neck decrease as set on next row and then on foll 6th row, ending with a RS row.
Work even in patt for 6 (8: 10) rows (Front should now match same length as Back to shoulder).
Fasten off.

TO FINISH

Press pieces lightly on wrong side, following instructions on yarn label.
Sew shoulder seams.
Sew side seams up to colored markers.

Front band and neckband

With RS facing and using size D-3 (3mm) hook, work edging along front opening edges and neck edge as follows:
Row 1 (RS) Join yarn with a sl st to first row-end at bottom of right front opening, ch 2, then working first sc in same place as sl st, work 2 sc in each "dc" row-end and 1 sc in each "sc" row-end up right front edge to shoulder, work 1 sc in each dc across back neck edge, then work 2 sc in each "dc" row-end and 1 sc in each "sc" row-end down left front edge, turn.
Row 2 Ch 2, skip first sc, *yo and insert hook in next sc, yo and draw a loop through sc and through first loop on hook, yo and draw through rem 2 loops on hook; rep from * to end, working last st in 2nd of 2-ch, turn.
Row 3 Ch 2, skip first st, *yo and insert hook in next st, yo and draw a loop through st and through first loop on hook, yo and draw through rem 2 loops on hook; rep from * to end, working last st in 2nd of 2-ch, turn.
Rep last row twice more.
Fasten off.

Sleeve edging

With RS facing, using size D-3 (3mm) hook, work edging along sleeve edge as follows:
Round 1 (RS) Join yarn with a sl st to first row-end on sleeve edge at side seam, then working first sc in same place as sl st, work 2 sc in each "dc" row-end and 1 sc in each "sc" row-end all around armhole, join with a sl st to first sc, do not turn.
Round 2 (RS) Ch 2, skip first sc, *yo and insert hook in next sc, yo and draw a loop through sc and through first loop on hook, yo and draw through rem 2 loops on hook; rep from * to end, working last st in 2nd of 2-ch.
Fasten off.
Sew row-end edges of front bands to skipped sts at center front. Sew on button.

COZY CONNIE SWEATER

See how lovely Connie looks in her Cozy Sweater with its sweet three-quarter-length sleeves. The simple textured stitch is very pretty and really quite easy to work. Connie is happy to wear it all day long as it is so warm and comfortable, and orange is her favorite color.

SIZES AND MEASUREMENTS

To fit ages (in years)	2–3	3–4	4–5
To fit chest	22in	24in	26in
	56cm	61cm	66cm
Finished measurements			
Around chest	26in	28in	30in
	66cm	71cm	76cm
Length to shoulder	14½in	15½in	16in
	37cm	39cm	41cm
Sleeve length	6½in	7½in	9in
	16cm	19cm	23cm

YARN

Rowan *Pure Wool DK* (1¾oz/50g balls) as follows:

A orange (Tangerine 040)	6 balls	7 balls	8 balls
B light turquoise (Pier 003)	1 ball	1 ball	1 ball

HOOKS

Size E-4 (3.5mm) crochet hook
Size G-6 (4mm) crochet hook

EXTRAS

1 button ⁷⁄₁₆in/11mm in diameter

GAUGE

20 sts and 24 rows to 4in/10cm measured over sc using size E-4 (3.5mm) crochet hook *or size necessary to obtain correct gauge.*

ABBREVIATIONS

sc2tog = [insert hook in next st, yo and draw a loop through] twice, yo and draw through all 3 loops on hook—*one st decreased.*
See also page 110.

UPPER BACK AND SLEEVES

Using size E-4 (3.5mm) hook and A, ch 67 (73: 79).

Foundation row (RS) 1 sc in 2nd ch from hook, 1 sc in each of rem ch, turn. *66 (72: 78) sc.*

Row 1 (patt row) Ch 1 (does NOT count as a st), 1 sc in each sc to end, turn.

(Last row forms simple sc patt when repeated.)

Cont in sc throughout, work 0 (2: 4) more rows, ending with a WS row.

Shape sleeves

Next row (RS) Ch 4 (5: 6), 1 sc in 2nd ch from hook, 1 sc in each of next 2 (3: 4) ch, 1 sc in each sc to end, turn.

Rep last row 5 times more, ending with a WS row. *84 (96: 108) sc.***

Work even until Back measures 6¼ (7: 7¾)in/ 16 (18: 20)cm from beg, ending with a WS row.

Shape upper sleeve, shoulder, and back neck

Next row (RS) 1 sl st in each of first 8 (9: 10) sc, ch 1, 1 sc in same sc as last sl st, 1 sc in each sc to last 7 (8: 9) sc, turn. *70 (80: 90) sc.*

Next row 1 sl st in each of first 8 (9: 10) sc, ch 1, 1 sc in same sc as last sl st, 1 sc in each of next 13 (16: 19) sc, work sc2tog over next 2 sc, 1 sc in next sc, turn. *16 (19: 22) sc.*

Working on these sts only for first side of neck, cont as follows:

Next row (RS) Ch 1, 1 sc in first sc, work sc2tog over next 2 sc, 1 sc in each of next 6 (8: 10) sc. *8 (10: 12) sc.*

Fasten off.

With WS facing, return to sts left unworked, skip center 22 (24: 26) sc and rejoin A with a sl st to next sc, ch 1, 1 sc in same sc as sl st, work sc2tog over next 2 sc, 1 sc in each of next 14 (17: 20) sc, turn. *16 (19: 22) sc.*

Next row 1 sl st in each of first 8 (9: 10) sc, ch 1, 1 sc in same sc as last sl st, 1 sc in each of next 5 (7: 9) sc, work sc2tog over next 2 sc, 1 sc in last sc. *8 (10: 12) sc.* Fasten off.

UPPER FRONT AND SLEEVES
Work as for Back to **.
Work even for 4 rows, ending with a WS row.

Divide for front opening
Next row (RS) Ch 1, 1 sc in each of first 41 (47: 53) sc, turn.
Working on these sts only for left side of front opening, cont as follows:
Work even until Front measures 4¼ (5: 6) in/ 11 (13: 15) cm from beg, ending with a WS row.

Shape left front neck
Next row (RS) Ch 1, 1 sc in each of first 32 (37: 42) sc, work sc2tog over next 2 sc, 1 sc in next sc, turn. 34 (39: 44) sc.
Next row Ch 1, 1 sc in first sc, work sc2tog over next 2 sc, 1 sc in each sc to end, turn.
Next row Ch 1, 1 sc in each sc to last 3 sc, work sc2tog over next 2 sc, 1 sc in last sc, turn.
Rep last 2 rows until 29 (34: 39) sc rem.
Work even until Front measures 6¼ (7: 7¾) in/ 16 (18: 20) cm from beg (same as Back to shoulder), ending with a WS row.

Shape left shoulder
Next row 1 sl st in each of first 8 (9: 10) sc, ch 1, 1 sc in same sc as last sl st, 1 sc in each sc to end, turn.
Next row Ch 1, 1 sc in each sc to last 7 (8: 9) sc, turn.
Next row 1 sl st in each of first 8 (9: 10) sc, ch 1, 1 sc in same sc as last sl st, 1 sc in each sc to end. 8 (10: 12) sc.
Fasten off.
With RS facing, return to sts left unworked, skip center 2 sc and rejoin A with a sl st to next sc, ch 1, 1 sc in same place as sl st, 1 sc in each sc to end, turn. 41 (47: 53) sc.
Work even until Front measures 4¼ (5: 6) in/ 11 (13: 15) cm from beg, ending with a WS row.

Shape right front neck
Next row (RS) 1 sl st in each of first 7 (8: 9) sc, ch 1, 1 sc in same place as last sl st, work sc2tog over next 2 sc, 1 sc in each sc to end, turn. 34 (39: 44) sc.
Next row Ch 1, 1 sc in each sc to last 3 sc, work sc2tog over next 2 sc, 1 sc in last sc, turn.

Next row Ch 1, 1 sc in first sc, work sc2tog over next 2 sc, 1 sc in each sc to end, turn.
Rep last 2 rows until 29 (34: 39) sc rem.
Work even until Front measures 6¼ (7: 7¾) in/ 16 (18: 20) cm from beg (same as Back to shoulder), ending with a WS row.

Shape right shoulder
Next row (RS) Ch 1, 1 sc in each sc to last 7 (8: 9) sc, turn.
Next row 1 sl st in each of first 8 (9: 10) sc, ch 1, 1 sc in same sc as last sl st, 1 sc in each sc to end, turn.
Next row Ch 1, 1 sc in each sc to last 7 (8: 9) sc, turn. 8 (10: 12) sc.
Fasten off.

LOWER BACK
With RS facing and using size E-4 (3.5mm) hook and A, work Lower Back along foundation-chain edge of Back as follows:
Foundation row (RS) Join A with a sl st to first foundation ch, ch 1, 1 sc in same place as sl st, 1 sc in each of next 33 (36: 39) ch, 2 sc in next ch, 1 sc in each of rem ch. 67 (73: 79) sc.
Patt row 1 Ch 2, [1 sc, 1 dc, 1 hdc] all in first sc, *skip next 2 sc, [1 sc, 1 dc, 1 hdc] all in next sc; rep from * to end, turn.
Patt row 2 Ch 2, *[1 sc, 1 dc, 1 hdc] all in next sc; rep from * to end, 1 sl st in 2nd of 2-ch, turn.
(Last row forms patt when repeated.)
Work in patt until work measures 9 (9¾ : 10½) in/ 23 (25: 27) cm from shoulder.
Change to size G-6 (4mm) hook.
Cont in patt until work measures 14½ (15½: 16) in/ 37 (39: 41) cm from shoulder, ending with a WS row.
Fasten off.

LOWER FRONT
Work Lower Front along foundation-chain edge of Front as for Lower Back.

LOWER SLEEVES (both alike)
Sew shoulder seams.
With RS facing and using size E-4 (3.5mm) hook and A, work Lower Sleeve along row-end edge of end of sleeve as follows:
Foundation row (RS) Join A with a sl st to first

row-end at end of sleeve, ch 1, 1 sc in same place as sl st, work 39 (45: 51) more sc evenly across row-ends. 40 (46: 52) sc.

Patt row 1 Ch 2, [1 sc, 1 dc, 1 hdc] all in first sc, *skip next 2 sc, [1 sc, 1 dc, 1 hdc] all in next sc; rep from * to end, turn.

Patt row 2 Ch 2, *[1 sc, 1 dc, 1 hdc] all in next sc; rep from * to end, 1 sl st in 2nd of 2-ch, turn. (Last row forms patt when repeated.)

Cont in patt until Lower Sleeve measures 2 (2½: 2¾) in/5 (6: 7) cm.

Change to size G-6 (4mm) hook.

Cont in patt for 2½ (2¾: 3) in/6 (7: 8) cm more, ending with a WS row.

Fasten off.

TO FINISH

Press pieces very lightly on wrong side, following instructions on yarn label.

Neck edging

With RS facing and using size E-4 (3.5mm) hook and B, work neck edging as follows:

Round 1 (RS) Join B with a sl st to neck edge at right shoulder seam, ch 1, 1 sc in same place as sl st, then work a row of sc evenly around neck edge, making a button loop of 6-ch 4 rows below neck edge on right front and working 2 sc in each corner at top of front opening and sc2tog at inner corners at base of front opening, join with a sl st to first sc.

Fasten off.

Sew side and sleeve seams.

Sew on button to correspond with button loop.

BESSIE BIRD COAT

Warm, woolly, cozy, practical, and fun, a Bessie Bird Coat is just what you need for playing outside in the winter. Keep it simple with just the colorful striped belt or make it truely lovely by decorating the pockets with two Bessie Birds. Either way, it looks good and is extra snug worn with the Winter Warmer hat and scarf on page 92.

BEFORE YOU BEGIN

SIZES AND MEASUREMENTS

To fit ages (in years)	2–3	3–4	4–5
To fit chest	22in	24in	26in
	56cm	61cm	66cm
Finished measurements			
Around chest	24¾in	26¾in	28¾in
	63cm	68cm	73cm
Length to shoulder	19in	21¾in	24½in
	48cm	55cm	62cm
Sleeve length	8½in	10in	11in
	22 cm	25cm	28cm

YARN

Rowan *Pure Wool DK* (1¾oz/50g balls) as follows:

A	red (Kiss 036)	8 balls	9 balls	10 balls
B	light turquoise (Pier 006)	1 ball	2 balls	2 balls
C	mid green (Parsley 020)	1 ball	1 ball	1 ball
D	yellow (Gilt 032)	1 ball	1 ball	1 ball

HOOK

Size E-4 (3.5mm) crochet hook

EXTRAS FOR BELT AND BIRD MOTIFS

1 buckle (for optional belt)
2 ecru buttons ⅜in/9mm in diameter, for optional bird motifs

GAUGE

25 sts and 21 rows to 4in/10cm measured over patt using size E-4 (3.5mm) crochet hook *or size necessary to obtain correct gauge.*

ABBREVIATIONS

sc2tog = [insert hook in next st, yo and draw a loop through] twice, yo and draw through all 3 loops on hook—*one st decreased.*
See also page 110.

GETTING STARTED

COAT

BACK

Using size E-4 (3.5mm) hook and B, ch 103 (113: 123).
Fasten off.
Change to A on next row as follows:
Foundation row (RS) Join A with a sl st to first ch, ch 1 (does NOT count as a st), 1 sc in same place as sl st, 1 sc in next ch, *ch 1, skip 1 ch, 1 sc in next ch; rep from * to last ch, 1 sc in last ch, turn. *103 (113: 123) sts—counting each sc and each 1-ch sp as a st.*
Patt row 1 Ch 1 (does NOT count as a st), 1 sc in first sc, *ch 1, 1 sc in next 1-ch sp; rep from * to last 2 sc, ch 1, 1 sc in last sc, turn.
Patt row 2 Ch 1, 1 sc in first sc, *1 sc in next 1-ch sp, ch 1; rep from * to last 1-ch sp, 1 sc in next 1-ch sp, 1 sc in last sc, turn.
(Last 2 rows form patt when repeated.)
Cont in patt as set throughout, work 7 (9: 11) rows more, ending with a WS row.
Next row (dec row) (RS) Ch 1, 1 sc in first sc, [1 sc in next 1-ch sp, ch 1] 5 times, work sc2tog over next 2 ch sps, work in patt to last 7 ch sps, work sc2tog over next 2 ch sps, [ch 1, 1 sc in next 1-ch sp] 5 times, 1 sc in last sc, turn. *(4 sts decreased.)*
Work even for 9 rows, ending with a WS row.
Rep last 10 rows 4 (5: 6) times more and then the dec row again. *79 (85: 91) sts.*
Work even until Back measures 13¾ (16: 18½)in/ 35 (41: 47)cm from beg, ending with a WS row.

Shape armholes

Next row (RS) 1 sl st in each of first 3 sts, ch 1, 1 sc in next 1-ch sp, work in patt to last 3 sts, turn. 73 *(79: 85)* sts.

Next row Ch 1, 1 sc in first sc, work sc2tog over next 2 ch sps, work in patt to last 2 ch sps, work sc2tog over next 2 ch sps, 1 sc in last sc, turn.

Next row Ch 1, 1 sc in first sc, ch 1, work sc2tog over next 2 ch sps, work in patt to last 2 ch sps, work sc2tog over next 2 ch sps, ch 1, 1 sc in last sc, turn.

Next row Ch 1, 1 sc in first sc, work sc2tog over next 2 ch sps, work in patt to last 2 ch sps, work sc2tog over next 2 ch sps, 1 sc in last sc, turn. 61 *(67: 73)* sts.

Work even until Back measures 17¾ (20½: 23¼) in/45 (52: 59) cm from beg, ending with a WS row.

Shape back neck

Next row (RS) Ch 1, 1 sc in first sc, [ch 1, 1 sc in next 1-ch sp] 8 (9: 10) times, turn. 17 *(19: 21)* sts. Working on these sts only for first side of neck, cont as follows:

Next row Ch 1, 1 sc in first sc, work sc2tog over next 2 ch sps, work in patt to end, turn.

Next row Work in patt to last 2 ch sps, work sc2tog over next 2 ch sps, ch 1, 1 sc in last sc, turn. 13 *(15: 17)* sts.

Work even for 3 rows.

Fasten off.

With RS facing, return to sts left unworked, skip center 27 (29: 31) sts and rejoin A with a sl st to next 1-ch sp, ch 1, 1 sc in same place as sl st, work in patt to end, turn. 17 *(19: 21)* sts.

Next row Work in patt to last 2 ch sps, work sc2tog over next 2 ch sps, 1 sc in last sc, turn.

Next row Ch 1, 1 sc in first sc, ch 1, work sc2tog over next 2 ch sps, work in patt to end, turn. 13 *(15: 17)* sts.

Work even for 3 rows.

Fasten off.

POCKET LININGS (make 2)

Using size E-4 (3.5mm) hook and B, ch 22 (24: 26).

Foundation row (RS) 1 sc in 2nd ch from hook, 1 sc in next ch, *ch 1, skip 1 ch, 1 sc in next ch; rep from * to last ch, 1 sc in last ch, turn. 21 *(23: 25)* sts.

Patt row 1 Ch 1 (does NOT count as a st), 1 sc in first sc, *ch 1, 1 sc in next 1-ch sp; rep from *

to last 2 sc, ch 1, 1 sc in last sc, turn.

Patt row 2 Ch 1, 1 sc in first sc, *1 sc in next 1-ch sp, ch 1; rep from * to last 1-ch sp, 1 sc in next 1-ch sp, 1 sc in last sc, turn.

(Last 2 rows form patt when repeated.)

Cont in patt as set, work 11 (13: 15) rows more.

Fasten off.

LEFT FRONT

Using size E-4 (3.5mm) hook and B, ch 55 (61: 67). Fasten off.

Change to A on next row as follows:

Foundation row (RS) Join A with a sl st to first ch, ch 1 (does NOT count as a st), 1 sc in same place as sl st, 1 sc in next ch, *ch 1, skip 1 ch, 1 sc in next ch; rep from * to last ch, 1 sc in last ch, turn. 55 *(61: 67)* sts.

Patt row 1 Ch 1 (does NOT count as a st), 1 sc in first sc, *ch 1, 1 sc in next 1-ch sp; rep from * to last 2 sc, ch 1, 1 sc in last sc, turn.

Patt row 2 Ch 1, 1 sc in first sc, *1 sc in next 1-ch sp, ch 1; rep from * to last 1-ch sp, 1 sc in next 1-ch sp, 1 sc in last sc, turn.

(Last 2 rows form patt when repeated.)

Cont in patt as set throughout, work 7 (9: 11) rows more, ending with a WS row.

Next row (dec row) (RS) Ch 1, 1 sc in first sc, [1 sc in next 1-ch sp, ch 1] 5 times, work sc2tog over next 2 ch sps, work in patt to end, turn. *(2 sts decreased.)*

Work even for 9 rows, ending with a WS row. Rep last 10 rows 2 (3: 4) times more and then the dec row again. 47 *(51: 55)* sts.

Work even for 5 rows, ending with a WS row.

Place pocket lining

Next row (RS) Ch 1, 1 sc in first sc, [1 sc in next 1-ch sp, ch 1] 8 (9: 10) times; then with RS of pocket lining facing WS of Front, work across pocket lining as follows—skip first sc, 1 sc in next 1-ch sp, [ch 1, 1 sc in next 1-ch sp] 9 (10: 11) times; skip 19 (21: 23) sts of Front, work in patt to end, turn. 47 *(51: 55)* sts.

Work even for 3 rows, ending with a WS row.

Next row (RS) Ch 1, 1 sc in first sc, [1 sc in next 1-ch sp, ch 1] 5 times, work sc2tog over next 2 ch sps, work in patt to end, turn. 45 *(49: 53)* sts.

Work even for 9 rows, ending with a WS row.

Next row (RS) Ch 1, 1 sc in first sc, [1 sc in next 1-ch sp, ch 1] 5 times, work sc2tog over next 2 ch sps, work in patt to end, turn. *43 (47: 51) sts.* Work even until Left Front measures 13¾ (16: 18½) in/35 (41: 47) cm from beg (same as Back to armhole), ending with a WS row.

Shape armhole
Next row (RS) 1 sl st in each of first 3 sts, ch 1, 1 sc in next 1-ch sp, work in patt to end. *40 (44: 48) sts.*
Next row Work in patt to last 2 ch sps, work sc2tog over next 2 ch sps, 1 sc in last sc, turn.
Next row Ch 1, 1 sc in first sc, ch 1, work sc2tog over next 2 ch sps, work in patt to end, turn.
Next row Work in patt to last 2 ch sps, work sc2tog over next 2 ch sps, 1 sc in last sc, turn. *34 (38: 42) sts.*
Work even until Left Front measures 15¾ (18½: 21¼) in/40 (47: 54) cm from beg, ending with a WS row.

Shape neck
Next row Ch 1, 1 sc in first sc, [ch 1, 1 sc in next 1-ch sp] 10 (11: 12) times, turn.
Next row Ch 1, 1 sc in first sc, work sc2tog over next 2 ch sps, work in patt to end, turn.
Next row Work in patt to last 2 ch sps, work sc2tog over next 2 ch sps, ch 1, 1 sc in last sc, turn.
Rep last 2 rows once more. *13 (15: 17) sts.*
Work even until Left Front measures same as Back to shoulder.
Fasten off.

RIGHT FRONT
Using size E-4 (3.5mm) hook and B, ch 55 (61: 67). Fasten off.
Change to A on next row as follows:
Foundation row (RS) Join A with a sl st to first ch, ch 1 (does NOT count as a st), 1 sc in same place as sl st, 1 sc in next ch, *ch 1, skip 1 ch, 1 sc in next ch; rep from * to last ch, 1 sc in last ch, turn. *55 (61: 67) sts.*
Patt row 1 Ch 1 (does NOT count as a st), 1 sc in first sc, *ch 1, 1 sc in next 1-ch sp; rep from * to last 2 sc, ch 1, 1 sc in last sc, turn.
Patt row 2 Ch 1, 1 sc in first sc, *1 sc in next 1-ch sp, ch 1; rep from * to last 1-ch sp, 1 sc in next 1-ch sp, 1 sc in last sc, turn.
(Last 2 rows form patt when repeated.)
Cont in patt as set throughout, work 7 (9: 11) rows more, ending with a WS row.
Next row (dec row) (RS) Work in patt to last 7 ch sps, work sc2tog over next 2 ch sps, [ch 1, 1 sc in next 1-ch sp] 5 times, 1 sc in last sc, turn. *(2 sts decreased.)*
Work even for 9 rows, ending with a WS row.
Rep last 10 rows 2 (3: 4) times more and then the dec row again. *47 (51: 55) sts.*
Work even for 5 rows, ending with a WS row.

Place pocket lining
Next row (RS) Ch 1, 1 sc in first sc, [1 sc in next 1-ch sp, ch 1] 5 times; then with RS of pocket lining facing WS of Front, work across pocket lining as follows—skip first sc, 1 sc in next 1-ch sp, [ch 1, 1 sc in next 1-ch sp] 9 (10: 11) times; skip 19 (21: 23) sts of Front, work in patt to end, turn. *47 (51: 55) sts.*
Work even for 3 rows, ending with a WS row.
Next row (RS) Work in patt to last 7 ch sps, work sc2tog over next 2 ch sps, [ch 1, 1 sc in next 1-ch sp] 5 times, 1 sc in last sc, turn. *45 (49: 53) sts.*
Work even for 9 rows, ending with a WS row.
Next row (RS) Work in patt to last 7 ch sps, work sc2tog over next 2 ch sps, [ch 1, 1 sc in next 1-ch sp] 5 times, 1 sc in last sc, turn. *43 (47: 51) sts.*
Work even until Right Front measures 13¾ (16: 18½) in/35 (41: 47) cm from beg (same as Back to armhole), ending with a WS row.

Shape armhole
Next row (RS) Work in patt to last 3 sts, turn. *40 (44: 48) sts.*
Next row Ch 1, 1 sc in first sc, work sc2tog over next 2 ch sps, work in patt to end, turn.
Next row Work in patt to last 2 ch sps, work sc2tog over next 2 ch sps, ch 1, 1 sc in last sc, turn.
Next row Ch 1, 1 sc in first sc, work sc2tog over next 2 ch sps, work in patt to end, turn. *34 (38: 42) sts.*
Work even until Right Front measures 15¾ (18½: 21¼) in/40 (47: 54) cm from beg, ending with a WS row.

Shape neck

Next row (RS) 1 sl st in each of first 13 (15: 17) sts, ch 1, 1 sc in next 1-ch sp, work in patt to end, turn.

Next row Work in patt to last 2 ch sps, work sc2tog over next 2 ch sps, 1 sc in last sc, turn.

Next row Ch 1, 1 sc in first sc, ch 1, work sc2tog over next 2 ch sps, work in patt to end, turn.

Rep last 2 rows once more. *13 (15: 17) sts.*

Work even until Right Front measures same as Back to shoulder.

Fasten off.

SLEEVES (make 2)

Using size E-4 (3.5mm) hook and B, ch 43 (47: 51). Fasten off.

Change to A on next row as follows:

Foundation row (RS) Join A with a sl st to first ch, ch 1 (does NOT count as a st), 1 sc in same place as sl st, 1 sc in next ch, *ch 1, skip 1 ch, 1 sc in next ch; rep from * to last ch, 1 sc in last ch, turn. *43 (47: 51) sts.*

Patt row 1 Ch 1 (does NOT count as a st), 1 sc in first sc, *ch 1, 1 sc in next ch sp; rep from * to last 2 sc, ch 1, 1 sc in last sc, turn.

Patt row 2 Ch 1, 1 sc in first sc, *1 sc in next 1-ch sp, ch 1; rep from * to last 1-ch sp, 1 sc in next 1-ch sp, 1 sc in last sc, turn.

(Last 2 rows form patt when repeated.)

Cont in patt as set throughout, work 1 row more.

Next row (inc row) (RS) Ch 1, 1 sc in first sc, [1 sc in next 1-ch sp, ch 1] 4 times, [1 sc, ch 1, 1 sc] all in next 1-ch sp, work in patt to last 5 ch sps, [1 sc, ch 1, 1 sc] all in next 1-ch sp, [ch 1, 1 sc in next 1-ch sp] 5 times, 1 sc in last sc. *(4 sts increased.)*

Work even for 5 rows, ending with a WS row.

Rep last 6 rows 5 (6: 7) times more and then the inc row again. *71 (79: 87) sts.*

Work even until Sleeve measures 8½ (10: 11) in/22 (25: 28) cm from beg, ending with a WS row.

Shape top of sleeve

Next row 1 sl st in each of first 3 sts, ch 1, 1 sc in next 1-ch sp, work in patt to last 3 sts, turn. *65 (73: 81) sts.*

Next row Ch 1, 1 sc in first sc, work sc2tog over next 2 ch sps, work in patt to last 2 ch sps, work sc2tog over next 2 ch sps, 1 sc in last sc, turn.

Next row Ch 1, 1 sc in first sc, ch 1, work sc2tog over next 2 ch sps, work in patt to last 2 ch sps, work sc2tog over next 2 ch sps, ch 1, 1 sc in last sc, turn.

Next row Ch 1, 1 sc in first sc, work sc2tog over next 2 ch sps, work in patt to last 2 ch sps, work sc2tog over next 2 ch sps, 1 sc in last sc, turn. *53 (61: 69) sts.*

Fasten off.

TO FINISH

Press pieces lightly on wrong side, following instructions on yarn label.

Sew shoulder seams.

Sew side seams. Sew sleeve seams and set in sleeves.

Sew pocket linings to wrong side of coat if bird motifs are not being made.

Edging

With RS facing and using size E-4 (3.5mm) hook and B, work edging around edge of coat as follows:

Round 1 (RS) Join B with a sl st to first row-end of Right Front at bottom edge of coat, then working up front edge, ch 1, 1 sc in same place as sl st, ch 1, skip first row-end, *1 sc in next row-end, ch 1,* rep from * to * to corner at neck edge, work [1 sc, ch 1, 1 sc] all into corner, cont working ch 1 and 1 sc alternately around neck edge to next corner, work [1 sc, ch 1, 1 sc] all into corner, work down Left Front in patt as set to corner, then working into other side of foundation ch, work [ch 1, 1 sc in next 1-ch sp] all along bottom edge of coat to beg of round, join with a sl st in first sc.

Do not turn work and do not fasten off.

Mark position for two buttonholes, 1¼ in/3cm and 4in/10cm from neck edge on Right Front, then cont edging up Right Front as follows:

Next row (RS) 1 sc in first 1-ch sp, **ch 1, 1 sc in next 1-ch sp,** rep from ** to ** to position of first buttonhole, ch 3, skip [1 sc, 1 ch and 1 sc], 1 sc in next 1-ch sp, rep from ** to ** to position of second buttonhole, ch 3, skip [1 sc, 1-ch and 1 sc], 1 sc in next 1-ch sp, cont in patt as set to

corner at neck edge, work [1 sc, ch 1, 1 sc] all in corner 1-ch sp, cont in patt to next corner, work [1 sc, ch 1, 1 sc] all in corner 1-ch sp, cont in patt to bottom of Left Front.
Fasten off.

BUTTONS (make 2)

Using size E-4 (3.5mm) hook and A, ch 2, leaving a long tail-end of yarn.
Round 1 (RS) 6 sc in 2nd ch from hook (working over tail-end of yarn), join with a sl st to first sc. (Do not turn work, but work with RS always facing.)
Round 2 Ch 1 (does NOT count as a st), 1 sc in each sc to end, join with a sl st to first sc. 6 sc.
Round 3 Ch 1, work sc2tog over first sc (same place as sl st) and next sc, [work sc2tog over next 2 sc] twice, join with a sl st to first sc. 3 sc.
Fasten off, leaving a long tail-end of yarn.
Pull long tail-end of yarn inside first round of sts

to close ring, then thread tail-end into center of button and use it to stuff button.
Use other tail-end to sew buttons to edge of Left Front to correspond with buttonholes.

BELT (optional)

TO MAKE BELT

The belt is made in two halves, that are joined together lengthwise along the center.

First half

Using size E-4 (3.5mm) hook and B, ch 160 (165: 170).
Fasten off, leaving a long tail-end of yarn.
Foundation row (RS) Using D, join yarn with a sl st to first ch, ch 1 (does NOT count as a st), 1 sc in same place as sl st, 1 sc in each of rem ch, turn. 160 (165: 170) sc.
Fasten off.

Row 1 Using C, join yarn with a sl st to first sc, ch 1 (does NOT count as a st), 1 sc in same place as sl st, 1 sc in each sc to end. Fasten off.

Second half

Work second half in same way as first half, but turn work at end of row 1 and do not fasten off C. Place first half behind second half with right sides of strips together and tops of last rows aligned, then still using C, join strips by working a row of sc through both pieces at once. Fasten off.

Edging at ends of belt

Using long tail-end of B, work a row of sc along each short end. Fasten off.

BELT LOOPS (make 3)

Using size E-4 (3.5mm) hook and A, ch 7.
Foundation row (RS) 1 sc in 2nd ch from hook, 1 sc in each of rem ch, turn. 6 sc.
Row 1 Ch 1 (does not count as a st), 1 sc in each sc to end.
Fasten off.

TO FINISH

Press pieces lightly on wrong side, following instructions on yarn label.
Sew buckle to one end of belt.
Sew one belt loop to each side seam and one to the center of the back. Thread belt through loops.

BIRD MOTIFS (optional)

BIRDS' BODIES 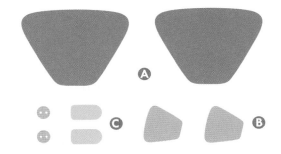 (make 2)

Using size E-4 (3.5mm) hook and C, ch 13.
Foundation row (RS) 1 sc in 2nd ch from hook, 1 sc in each of rem ch, turn. *12 sc.*
Row 1 (patt row) Ch 1 (does NOT count as a st), 1 sc in each sc to end, turn.
(Last row forms simple sc patt when repeated.)
Cont in sc throughout, work 3 rows more.
Next row (dec row) Ch 1, 1 sc in first sc, work sc2tog over next 2 sc, 1 sc in each sc to last 3 sc, work sc2tog over next 2 sc, 1 sc in last sc, turn.
Work even for 1 row.

Rep dec row twice. 6 sc.
Next row Ch 1, 1 sc in first sc, [work sc2tog over next 2 sc] twice, 1 sc in last sc. 4 sc.
Fasten off.

WINGS 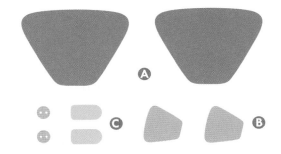 (make 2)

Using size E-4 (3.5mm) hook and B, ch 5.
Foundation row (RS) 1 sc in 2nd ch from hook, 1 sc in each of rem ch, turn. 4 sc.
Row 1 Ch 1 (does NOT count as a st), 1 sc in each sc to end, turn.
Row 2 Ch 1, [work sc2tog over next 2 sc] twice, turn. 2 sc.
Row 3 Ch 1, 1 sc in each of 2 sc.
Fasten off.

BEAKS 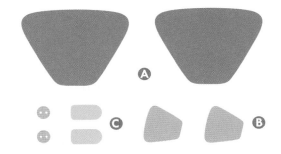 (make 2)

Using size E-4 (3.5mm) hook and D, ch 4.
Foundation row (RS) 1 sc in 2nd ch from hook, 1 sc in each of rem 2 ch. 3 sc.
Fasten off.

TO FINISH

Press pieces lightly on wrong side, following instructions on yarn label.
Using a blunt-ended yarn needle, embroider each bird body with two French knots in B and two in D as shown (see page 76).
Sew a beak and a wing to each bird, then sew on a button for the eye.
Sew one bird to front of each pocket, leaving beaks free.
Using B, embroider two legs below bird as shown. Using D, work three short even stitches fanning out from bird for tail, then work a French knot in B at the end of each stitch.
Sew pocket linings to wrong side of coat.

MILO OWL SWEATER

Boys will love this sturdy little sweater with its simple striped sleeves, simple embroidery, and, of course, Milo. It is very easily made in single crochet and is ideal for keeping warm all winter. Try wearing it with the Winter Warmer scarf on page 93—so cozy!

Try wearing it with the Winter Warmer scarf on page 93—so cozy!

BEFORE YOU BEGIN

SIZES AND MEASUREMENTS

To fit ages in years	2–3	3–4	4–5
To fit chest	22in	24in	26in
	56cm	61cm	66cm
Finished measurements			
Around chest	29in	31in	33in
	74cm	79cm	84cm
Length to shoulder	14½in	15¼in	16in
	37cm	39cm	41cm
Sleeve length	8¼in	10¼in	11½in
	21cm	26cm	29cm

YARN

Rowan *Pure Wool DK* (1¾oz/50g balls) as follows:

A	dark gray (Anthracite 003)	6 balls	7 balls	8 balls
B	mid green (Parsley 020)	1 ball	2 balls	2 balls
C	light turquoise (Pier 006)	1 ball	2 balls	2 balls

HOOK

Size E-4 (3.5mm) crochet hook

EXTRAS

2 red buttons ⁷⁄₁₆in/11mm in diameter, for owl's eyes

GAUGE

20 sts and 24 rows to 4in/10cm measured over sc using size E-4 (3.5mm) crochet hook *or size necessary to obtain correct gauge.*

ABBREVIATIONS

sc2tog = [insert hook in next st, yo and draw a loop through] twice, yo and draw through all 3 loops on hook—*one st decreased.*
See also page 110.

GETTING STARTED

SWEATER

BACK

Using size E-4 (3.5mm) hook and A, ch 75 (80: 85).

Foundation row (RS) 1 sc in 2nd ch from hook, 1 sc in each of rem ch, turn. *74 (79: 84) sc.*

Row 1 (patt row) Ch 1 (does NOT count as a st), 1 sc in each sc to end, turn.

(Last row forms simple sc patt when repeated.)
Work 1 (3: 5) rows more in sc.
Cont in sc throughout, work 1 row in B, then 1 row in C.
Cut off B and C.
Cont in A, work until Back measures 8¾ (9: 9½) in/ 22 (23: 24) cm from beg, ending with a WS row.

Shape armholes

Next row (RS) 1 sl st in each of first 6 (7: 8) sc, ch 1, 1 sc same place as last sl st, 1 sc in each sc to last 5 (6: 7) sc, turn. *64 (67: 70) sc.*

Next row Ch 1, 1 sc in first sc, work sc2tog over next 2 sc, 1 sc in each sc to last 3 sc, work sc2tog over next 2 sc, 1 sc in last sc, turn.

Rep last row twice more, ending with a WS row. *58 (61: 64) sc.***

Work even until Back measures 14 (15: 15¾) in/ 36 (38: 40) cm from beg, ending with a WS row.

Shape back neck

Next row (RS) Ch 1, 1 sc in each of first 15 (16: 17) sc, work sc2tog over next 2 sc, 1 sc in next sc, turn. *17 (18: 19) sc.*

Working on these sts only for first side of neck, cont as follows:

Next row Ch 1, 1 sc in first sc, work sc2tog over next 2 sc, 1 sc in each sc to end, turn. *16 (17: 18) sc.*

Next row Ch 1, 1 sc in each sc to last 3 sc, work sc2tog over next 2 sc, 1 sc in last sc. *15 (16: 17) sc.*

Fasten off.

With RS facing, return to sts left unworked, skip

center 22 (23: 24) sc and rejoin A with a sl st to next sc, ch 1, 1 sc in same place as sl st, work sc2tog over next 2 sc, 1 sc in each sc to end, turn. *17 (18: 19) sc.*

Next row Ch 1, 1 sc in each sc to last 3 sc, work sc2tog over next 2 sc, 1 sc in last sc, turn. *16 (17: 18) sc.*

Next row Ch 1, 1 sc in first sc, work sc2tog over next 2 sc, 1 sc in each sc to end. *15 (16: 17) sc.*
Fasten off.

FRONT

Work as for Back to **.
Work even for 8 rows, ending with a WS row.

Shape front neck

Next row (RS) Ch 1, 1 sc in each of first 23 (24: 25) sc, work sc2tog over next 2 sc, 1 sc in next sc, turn. *25 (26: 27) sc.*
Working on these sts only for first side of neck, cont as follows:
Next row Ch 1, 1 sc in each sc to end, turn.
Next row Ch 1, 1 sc in each sc to last 3 sc, work sc2tog over next 2 sc, 1 sc in last sc, turn.
Rep last 2 rows until 15 (16: 17) sc rem.
Work even until Front measures same as Back to shoulder.
Fasten off.
With RS facing, return to sts left unworked, skip center 6 (7: 8) sc and rejoin A with a sl st to next sc, ch 1, 1 sc in same place as sl st, work sc2tog over next 2 sc, 1 sc in each sc to end, turn. *25 (26: 27) sc.*
Next row Ch 1, 1 sc in each sc to end, turn.
Next row Ch 1, 1 sc in first sc, work sc2tog over next 2 sc, 1 sc in each sc to end, turn.
Rep last 2 rows until 15 (16: 17) sc rem.
Work even until Front measures same as Back to shoulder.
Fasten off.

SLEEVES (make 2)

Using size E-4 (3.5mm) hook and A, ch 37 (39: 41).
Foundation row (RS) 1 sc in 2nd ch from hook, 1 sc in each of rem ch, turn. *36 (38: 40) sc.*
Row 1 (patt row) Ch 1 (does NOT count as a st), 1 sc in each sc to end, turn.

(Last row forms simple sc patt when repeated.)
Work 1 row more in sc.
Cont in sc throughout, work 1 row in B, then 1 row in C.
Cont in stripe sequence of [3 rows A, 3 rows B, 3 rows C] repeated throughout *and at the same time* shape Sleeve as follows:
Work 1 row.
Next row (inc row) (RS) Ch 1, 1 sc in each of first 4 sc, 2 sc in next sc, 1 sc in each sc to last 5 sc, 2 sc in next sc, 1 sc in each of last 4 sc, turn. *(2 sc increased.)*
Work even for 3 rows.
Rep last 4 rows 9 (11: 12) times more and then the inc row again. *58 (64: 68) sc.*
Work even for 3 (7: 11) rows, ending with 3 (3: 2) rows C (A: A).
Mark each end of last row with a colored thread.
Work even for 6 (7: 8) rows more.

Shape top of sleeve

Next row Ch 1, 1 sc in first sc, work sc2tog over next 2 sc, 1 sc in each sc to last 3 sc, work sc2tog over next 2 sc, 1 sc in last sc, turn.
Rep last row twice more. *52 (58: 62) sc.*
Fasten off.

TO FINISH

Press pieces lightly on wrong side, following instructions on yarn label.
Sew shoulder seams.

Neck edging

With RS facing and using size E-4 (3.5mm) hook, work edging along neck as follows:
Round 1 (RS) Using A, join yarn with a sl st to neck edge at right shoulder seam, ch 1, 1 sc in same place as sl st, then work a round of sc evenly around neck edge, join with a sl st to first sc.
Fasten off.
Turn work and with WS facing, join in B on next round as follows:
Round 2 (WS) Using B, join yarn with a sl st to last sc at end of last round, ch 1, 1 sc in same place as sl st, 1 sc in each sc to end of round, join with a sl st to first sc.
Fasten off.

Turn work and with RS facing, join in C on next round as follows:

Round 3 (RS) Using C, join yarn with a sl st to last sc at end of last round, ch 1, 1 sc in same place as sl st, 1 sc in each sc to 1 sc before first of two corners on center front neck, work sc2tog over next 2 sc (to shape corner), 1 sc in each sc to 1 sc before second corner, work sc2tog over next 2 sc, 1 sc in each sc to end of round, join with a sl st to first sc.
Fasten off.
Sew sleeves to armholes, stitching rows above colored markers to armhole shaping on Front and Back. Sew side and sleeve seams.

Embroidery

Using a blunt-ended yarn needle and B, embroider a cross-stitch over every alt sc all around sweater, one row up from stripe in C at lower edge.

On Front, skip one row of sc above row of cross-stitches and embroider four cross-stitches in same way above center four cross-stitches below, then skip one row of sc and embroider three cross-stitches centered above last four.

OWL MOTIF

OWL'S BODY Ⓐ

Using size E-4 (3.5mm) hook and C, ch 9.
Foundation row (RS) 1 sc in 2nd ch from hook, 1 sc in each of rem ch, turn. *8 sc.*
Row 1 (patt row) Ch 1 (does NOT count as a st), 1 sc in each sc to end, turn.
(Last forms simple sc patt when repeated.)
Row 2 Ch 1, 1 sc in first sc, 2 sc in next sc, 1 sc in each of next 4 sc, 2 sc in next sc, 1 sc in last sc, turn. *10 sc.*
Row 3 Rep row 1.
Row 4 Ch 1, 1 sc in first sc, 2 sc in next sc, 1 sc in each of next 6 sc, 2 sc in next sc, 1 sc in last sc, turn. *12 sc.*
Cont in sc throughout, work even for 7 rows, ending with a WS row.
Next row (dec row) (RS) Ch 1, 1 sc in first sc, work sc2tog over next 2 sc, 1 sc in each sc to last 3 sc, work sc2tog over next 2 sc, 1 sc in last sc, turn. *10 sc.*

Rep last row twice more. *6 sc.*

Shape ears
Next row (WS) Ch 1, 1 sc in each of first 2 sc, turn. *2 sc.*
Working on these sts only for first ear, cont as follows:
**Next row Ch 1, 1 sc in each sc to end, turn.
Next row Ch 1, work sc2tog over first 2 sc. *1 sc.*
Fasten off.**
With WS facing, skip center 2 sc and rejoin C with a sl st to next sc, ch 1, 1 sc in same place as sl st, 1 sc in last sc, turn. *2 sc.*
Complete as for first ear from ** to **.

OWL'S WINGS Ⓑ (make 2)

Using size E-4 (3.5mm) hook and C, ch 6.
Round 1 (RS) 1 sc in 2nd ch from hook, 1 sc in each of next 4 ch, then working along other side of foundation ch, work 1 sc in each of next 5 ch, 4 dc in same place as last sc, 1 sl st in same place as 4 dc.
Fasten off.

OWL'S BEAK Ⓒ

Using size E-4 (3.5mm) hook and A, ch 5.
Foundation row (RS) 1 sc in 2nd ch from hook, 1 sc in each of rem 3 ch. *4 sc.*
Fasten off, leaving a long tail-end of yarn.

TO FINISH

Press pieces lightly on wrong side, following instructions on yarn label.

Wings, eyes, and beak
With 4-dc group at bottom of wing, sew top of

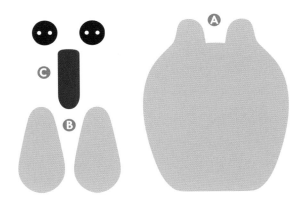

one side of each wing to owl's body as shown (see page 86).

For eyes, sew on two buttons as shown, using A. Sew one end of beak to owl's body between eyes.

Embroidery

Using a blunt-ended yarn needle, work embroidery as follows:

Using B, sew two vertical straight stitches at center of each ear.

Using A, sew three straight stitches fanning out downward from the same point to form feet at lower end of owl's body.

Using B, embroider four cross-stitches across center of owl's body, leaving one sc free between them (position them six rows up from lower edge, and over two rows vertically and 1 sc horizontally).

Skip a row of sc and using B, work three smaller cross-stitches (over only one row vertically) below the first four.

Using A, work a short horizontal stitch across center of each cross-stitch.

Leaving wings and ears free, sew owl to sweater above cross-stitches at center of Front.

WINTER WARMERS

Boys and girls can play outside all day when they are wearing their Winter Warmers. Easily made, the hat is snug with cozy earflaps and the scarf is extremely warm because it is folded to make it double thickness. Enjoy the winter weather!

BEFORE YOU BEGIN

SIZES AND MEASUREMENTS

To fit ages (in years)	2–3	3–4	4–5
Finished hat measurements			
Circumference	17½in	18in	19in
	44cm	46cm	48cm
Length from center top,	6½in	7¼in	8in
excluding flaps	17cm	18.5cm	20cm

Scarf size
The finished scarf measures 6in/15cm by 27½in/70cm.

YARN

Rowan *Pure Wool DK* (1¾oz/50g balls) as follows:

Girl's Hat and Scarf

A	red (Kiss 036)	2 balls	2 balls	2 balls
B	light turquoise (Pier 006)	1 ball	1 ball	1 ball
C	mid green (Parsley 020)	1 ball	1 ball	1 ball

Boy's Hat and Scarf

A	dark gray (Anthracite 003)	1 ball	1 ball	1 ball
B	light turquoise (Pier 006)	1 ball	1 ball	1 ball
C	mid green (Parsley 020)	1 ball	1 ball	1 ball

Note: If you are making only either the hat or the scarf, you will need only one ball of each of the three colors.

HOOK
Size G-6 (4mm) crochet hook

EXTRAS FOR SCARF
2 large snaps
1 button ⅞in/22mm in diameter

GAUGE
16½ sts and 22 rows to 4in/10cm measured over sc using size G-6 (4mm) crochet hook *or size necessary to obtain correct gauge.*

ABBREVIATIONS
sc2tog = [insert hook in next st, yo and draw a loop through] twice, yo and draw through all 3 loops on hook—*one st decreased.*
See also page 110.

GETTING STARTED

HAT

TO MAKE HAT
The hat is worked starting at the top.
Using size G-6 (4mm) hook and A, ch 17.
Foundation round (WS) Using A, 1 sc in 2nd ch from hook, 1 sc in each ch to last ch, 2 sc in last ch, then working along other side of foundation ch, skip first ch, 1 sc in each ch to end of this side of foundation ch, change to B and join with a sl st to first ch, turn. 32 sc.
(Remember to turn the work at the end of each round.)
Round 1 (RS) Using B, ch 1 (does NOT count as a st), 2 sc in first sc, 1 sc in each of next 14 sc, 2 sc in each of next 2 sc, 1 sc in each of next 14 sc, 2 sc in last sc, change to C and join with a sl st to first ch, turn. 36 sc.
Round 2 Using C, ch 1, 2 sc in first sc, 1 sc in each of next 16 sc, 2 sc in each of next 2 sc, 1 sc in each of next 16 sc, 2 sc in last sc, change to A and join with a sl st to first ch, turn. 40 sc.
Round 3 Using A, ch 1, 2 sc in first sc, 1 sc in each of next 18 sc, 2 sc in each of next 2 sc, 1 sc in each of next 18 sc, 2 sc in last sc, join with a sl st to first ch, turn. 44 sc.
Round 4 Using A, ch 1, 2 sc in first sc, 1 sc in each of next 20 sc, 2 sc in each of next 2 sc, 1 sc in each of next 20 sc, 2 sc in last sc, change to B and join with a sl st to first ch, turn. 48 sc.
These 4 rounds form the stripe sequence of [1 row B, 1 row C, 2 rows A] repeated and set the positions for the increases.
Cont as now set with stripe sequence and increases (increasing 4 sts in each round) for 4 rounds more. 64 sc.

Keeping stripe sequence correct as set throughout, cont as follows:

Next round (patt round) Using correct color, ch 1 (does NOT count as a st), 1 sc in each sc to to end of round, then using correct color join with a sl st to first ch, turn.

Increase as set on next round and then on foll alt round 1 (2: 3) times. *72 (76: 80) sc.*

Rep patt round until hat measures 6½ (7¼: 8) in/ 17 (18.5: 20) cm from foundation ch, ending with 2 rounds in A and a WS row.

Fasten off.

Cut off B and C.

First earflap

With RS facing and using size G-6 (4mm) hook and A, beg first earflap on next row as follows:

Next row (RS) Skip first 26 (27: 28) sc after fasten-off point and rejoin A with a sl st to next sc, ch 1, 1 sc in same place as sl st, 1 sc in each of next 10 (11: 12) sc, turn. *11 (12: 13) sc.*

Working on these sts only for first earflap, cont as follows:

**Next row Ch 1, 1 sc in each sc to end, turn.

Rep last row 3 (5: 7) times more.

Next row Ch 1, 1 sc in first sc, work sc2tog over next 2 sc, 1 sc in each sc to last 3 sc, work sc2tog over next 2 sc, 1 sc in last sc, turn.

Next row Ch 1, 1 sc in each sc to end, turn.

Rep last 2 rows twice more. *5 (6: 7) sc.*

Next row Ch 1, work sc2tog over first 2 sc, 1 sc in each of next 1 (2: 3) sc, work sc2tog over last 2 sc. *3 (4: 5) sc.*

Fasten off.**

94

Second earflap

With RS facing and using size G-6 (4mm) hook and A, beg second earflap on next row as follows:

Next row (RS) Skip 24 (25: 26) sc after last earflap and rejoin A with a sl st to next sc, ch 1, 1 sc in same place as sl st, 1 sc in each of next 10 (11: 12) sc, turn. *11 (12: 13) sc.*
Working on these sts only for second earflap, work as for first earflap from ** to **.

TO FINISH

Press lightly on wrong side, following instructions on yarn label.

Edging

With RS facing and using size G-6 (4mm) hook and B, join yarn with a sl st to a sc at center back of hat, ch 1, 1 sc in same place as sl st, then work a row of sc evenly all around outside edge of hat, join with a sl st to first sc.
Fasten off.

SCARF

TO MAKE SCARF

Using size G-6 (4mm) hook and A, ch 95.
Foundation round (WS) Ch 1, 1 sc in 2nd ch from hook, 1 sc in each sc to last ch, 2 sc in last ch, then working along other side of foundation ch, skip first ch, 1 sc in each ch to end of this side of foundation ch, change to B and join with a sl st to first ch, turn. *188 sc.*
(Remember to turn the work at the end of each round.)

1st round (RS) Using B, ch 1 (does NOT count as a st), 2 sc in first sc, 1 sc in each of next 92 sc, 2 sc in each of next 2 sc, 1 sc in each of next 92 sc, 2 sc in last sc, change to C and join with a sl st to first ch, turn. *(4 sts increased.)*

2nd round Using C, ch 1, 2 sc in first sc, 1 sc in each of next 94 sc, 2 sc in each of next 2 sc, 1 sc in each of next 94 sc, 2 sc in last sc, change to A and join with a sl st to first ch, turn. *(4 sts increased.)*

3rd round Using A, ch 1, 2 sc in first sc, 1 sc in each of next 96 sc, 2 sc in each of next 2 sc, 1 sc in each of next 96 sc, 2 sc in last sc, join with

a sl st to first ch, turn. *(4 sts increased.)*

4th round Using A, ch 1, 2 sc in first sc, 1 sc in each of next 98 sc, 2 sc in each of next 2 sc, 1 sc in each of next 98 sc, 2 sc in last sc, change to B and join with a sl st to first ch, turn. *(4 sts increased.)*

These 4 rounds form the stripe sequence of [1 row B, 1 row C, 2 rows A] repeated and set the positions for the increases.
Cont as now set with stripe sequence and increases (increasing 4 sts in each round) for 13 rounds more, ending with one round in B. Fasten off.

TO FINISH

Press lightly on wrong side, following instructions on yarn label.
Fold scarf in half lengthwise with wrong sides together and sew together around outside edge.
Sew on two snaps where scarf crosses as shown (see page 93).
Sew button on top of snaps for decoration.

HENRI ELEPHANT

Henri is happiest when he can stand quietly under shady trees with his friend and listen to parrots and monkeys singing. Try making him in different colors—he is very quick and easy to crochet. He prefers to wear his blanket, winter or summer, as he is particularly fond of stars.

BEFORE YOU BEGIN

SIZE
The finished toy elephant measures approximately 8in/20.5cm long by 6½in/16.5cm tall.

YARN
Rowan *Pure Wool DK* (1¾oz/50g balls) as follows:

Green Elephant
A	light green (Avocado 019)	2 balls
B	light turquoise (Pier 006)	1 ball
C	red (Kiss 036)	1 ball
D	steel blue (Cypress 007)	1 ball

Blue Elephant
A	steel blue (Cypress 007)	2 balls
B	light turquoise (Pier 006)	1 ball
C	gold (Honey 033)	1 ball
D	red (Kiss 036)	1 ball

HOOK
Size E-4 (3.5mm) crochet hook

EXTRAS
2 small buttons ⁷⁄₁₆in/11mm in diameter
Washable stuffing

GAUGE
20 sts and 24 rows to 4in/10cm measured over sc using size E-4 (3.5mm) crochet hook *or size necessary to obtain correct gauge.*

ABBREVIATIONS
sc2tog = [insert hook in next st, yo and draw a loop through] twice, yo and draw through all 3 loops on hook—*one st decreased.*
See also page 110.

BODY—LEFT SIDE Ⓐ
Each side of the elephant's body is worked from the top of the back to the feet.
Using size E-4 (3.5mm) hook and A, ch 21.
Foundation row (RS) 1 sc in 2nd ch from hook, 1 sc in each of rem ch, turn. *20 sc.*
Row 1 Ch 1 (does NOT count as a st), 2 sc in each of first 2 sc, 1 sc in each sc to last 2 sc, 2 sc in each of last 2 sc, turn. *24 sc.*
To help keep track of which is RS of piece, after turning work and before beg next row, mark this side of work as RS with a colored thread.
Row 2 (RS) Rep row 1. *28 sc.*
Row 3 Ch 1, 2 sc in first sc, 1 sc in each sc to last 2 sc, 2 sc in each of last 2 sc, turn. *31 sc.*
Row 4 Ch 1, 2 sc in first sc, 1 sc in each sc to last sc, 2 sc in last sc, turn. *33 sc.*
Rows 5 and 6 [Rep row 4] twice. *37 sc.*
Row 7 Ch 1, 1 sc in each sc to last sc, 2 sc in last sc, turn. *38 sc.*
Row 8 Rep row 4. *40 sc.*
Row 9 Ch 1, 1 sc in each sc to end, turn.
Row 10 Rep row 4. *42 sc.*
Row 11 Rep row 9.
Row 12 Ch 1, 2 sc in first sc, 1 sc in each sc to end, turn. *43 sc.*
Row 13 Rep row 9.
Row 14 Rep row 12. *44 sc.*
Row 15 Rep row 9.
Row 16 Rep row 12. *45 sc.*
Rows 17–21 [Rep row 9] 5 times.

Trunk
Row 22 (RS) Ch 1, 1 sc in each of first 8 sc, turn. *8 sc.*
Working on these sts only for trunk, cont as follows:
Row 23 Ch 1, 1 sc in first sc, work sc2tog over next 2 sc, 1 sc in each sc to end, turn. *7 sc.*
Rows 24–30 [Rep row 9] 7 times.
Fasten off.

Body

With RS facing, cont with body by rejoining A to sts left unworked as follows:

Row 22 (RS) Skip next sc and rejoin A with a sl st to next sc, ch 1, 1 sc in same place as sl st, 1 sc in each sc to end, turn. *36 sc.*

Row 23 Ch 1, 1 sc in each sc to last 3 sc, work sc2tog over next 2 sc, 1 sc in last sc, turn. *35 sc.*

Rows 24 and 25 [Rep row 9] twice.

Front leg

Row 26 (RS) Ch 1, 1 sc in each of first 12 sc, turn. *12 sc.*

Working on these sts only for front leg, cont as follows:

Row 27 Ch 1, 1 sc in first sc, work sc2tog over next 2 sc, 1 sc in each sc to end, turn. *11 sc.*

Row 28 Ch 1, 1 sc in each sc to last 3 sc, work sc2tog over next 2 sc, 1 sc in last sc, turn. *10 sc.*

Rows 29–35 [Rep row 9] 7 times. Fasten off.

Back leg

With RS facing, work back leg by rejoining A to sts left unworked as follows:

Row 26 (RS) Skip next 11 sc, rejoin A with a sl st to next sc, ch 1, 1 sc in first same place as sl st, 1 sc in each of last 11 sc, turn. *12 sc.*

Row 27 Ch 1, 1 sc in each sc to last 3 sc, work sc2tog over next 2 sc, 1 sc in last sc, turn. *11 sc.*

Row 28 Ch 1, 1 sc in first sc, work sc2tog over next 2 sc, 1 sc in each sc to end, turn. *10 sc.*

Rows 29–35 [Rep row 9] 7 times. Fasten off.

BODY—RIGHT SIDE Ⓑ

Using size E-4 (3.5mm) hook and A, ch 21.

Foundation row (RS) 1 sc in 2nd ch from hook,

1 sc in each of rem ch, turn. 20 sc.

Row 1 Ch 1 (does NOT count as a st), 2 sc in each of first 2 sc, 1 sc in each sc to last 2 sc, 2 sc in each of last 2 sc, turn. 24 sc.

To help keep track of which is RS of piece, after turning work and before beg next row, mark this side of work as RS with a colored thread.

Row 2 (RS) Rep row 1. 28 sc.

Row 3 Ch 1, 2 sc in each of first 2 sc, 1 sc in each sc to last sc, 2 sc in last sc, turn. 31 sc.

Row 4 Ch 1, 2 sc in first sc, 1 sc in each sc to last sc, 2 sc in last sc, turn. 33 sc.

Rows 5 and 6 [Rep row 4] twice. 37 sc.

Row 7 Ch 1, 2 sc in first sc, 1 sc in each sc to end, turn. 38 sc.

Row 8 Rep row 4. 40 sc.

Row 9 Ch 1, 1 sc in each sc to end, turn.

Row 10 Rep row 4. 42 sc.

Row 11 Rep row 9.

Row 12 Ch 1, 1 sc in each sc to last sc, 2 sc in last sc, turn. 43 sc.

Row 13 Rep row 9.

Row 14 Rep row 12. 44 sc.

Row 15 Rep row 9.

Row 16 Rep row 12. 45 sc.

Rows 17–21 [Rep row 9] 5 times.

Legs

Row 22 (RS) Ch 1, 1 sc in each of first 36 sc, turn. 36 sc.

Working on these sts only for legs section, cont as follows:

Row 23 Ch 1, 1 sc in first sc, work sc2tog over next 2 sc, 1 sc in each sc to end, turn. 35 sc.

Rows 24 and 25 [Rep row 9] twice.

Back leg

Row 26 Ch 1, 1 sc in each of first 12 sc, turn. 12 sc.

Working on these sts only for back leg, cont as follows:

Row 27 Ch 1, 1 sc in first sc, work sc2tog over next 2 sc, 1 sc in each sc to end, turn. 11 sc.

Row 28 Ch 1, 1 sc in each sc to last 3 sc, work sc2tog over next 2 sc, 1 sc in last sc, turn. 10 sc.

Rows 29–35 [Rep row 9] 7 times.

Fasten off.

Front leg

With RS facing, work front leg by rejoining A to sts left unworked as follows:

Row 26 (RS) Skip next 11 sc and rejoin A with a sl st to next sc, ch 1, 1 sc in same place as sl st, 1 sc in each of next 11 sc, turn. 12 sc.

Working on these sts only for front leg, cont as follows:

Row 27 Ch 1, 1 sc in each sc to last 3 sc, work sc2tog over next 2 sc, 1 sc in last sc, turn. 11 sc.

Row 28 Ch 1, 1 sc in first sc, work sc2tog over next 2 sc, 1 sc in each sc to end, turn. 10 sc.

Rows 29–35 [Rep row 9] 7 times.

Fasten off.

Trunk

With RS facing, work trunk by rejoining A to sts left unworked as follows:

Row 22 (RS) Skip next sc and rejoin A with a sl st to next sc, ch 1, 1 sc in same place as sl st, 1 sc in each sc to end, turn. 8 sc.

Row 23 Ch 1, 1 sc in each sc to last 3 sc, work sc2tog over next 2 sc, 1 sc in last sc, turn. 7 sc.

Rows 24–30 [Rep row 9] 7 times.

Fasten off.

UNDERBODY ⓒ

The underbody forms the belly, the insides of the legs and the underside of the trunk, and it is worked from the back legs to the trunk.

Inside of back legs

Using size E-4 (3.5mm) hook and A, ch 31.

Foundation row (RS) 1 sc in 2nd ch from hook, 1 sc in each of rem ch, turn. 30 sc.

Row 1 (patt row) Ch 1 (does NOT count as a st), 1 sc in each sc to end, turn.

(Last row forms simple sc patt when repeated.)

Cont in sc throughout, work 8 rows more, ending with a WS row.

Fasten off.

Shape belly

With RS facing, rejoin A and shape belly as follows:

Next row (RS) Skip first 8 sc and rejoin A with a sl st to next sc, ch 1, 1 sc in same place as sl st, 1 sc in each of next 13 sc, turn. 14 sc.

Next row Ch 1, work sc2tog over first 2 sc, 1 sc

in each sc to last 2 sc, work sc2tog over last 2 sc, turn.

Rep last row once more. *10 sc.*

Work even for 10 rows, ending with a RS row.

Next row (WS) Ch 1, 2 sc in first sc, 1 sc in each sc to last sc, 2 sc in last sc, turn. *12 sc.*

Next row Ch 1, 2 sc in first sc, 1 sc in each sc to last sc, 2 sc in last sc, turn. *14 sc.*

Do not cut off yarn or fasten off, but set aside while you make a length of ch for one leg.

Inside of front legs

Using size E-4 (3.5mm) hook and a separate length of A, ch 8 for front leg.

Fasten off.

Return to belly and cont as follows:

Next row (WS) Ch 9, 1 sc in 2nd ch from hook, 1 sc in each of rem 7 ch, 1 sc in each sc to end, then work 1 sc in each of 8 ch just made. *30 sc.*

Work even for 9 rows, ending with a RS row.

Fasten off.

Shape trunk

With WS facing, rejoin A and work trunk as follows:

Next row (WS) Skip first 13 sc and rejoin A with a sl st to next sc, ch 1, 1 sc in same place as sl st, 1 sc in each of next 3 sc, turn. *4 sc.*

Work even for 4 rows.

Next row Ch 1, [work sc2tog over next 2 sc] twice, turn. *2 sc.*

Work even for 6 rows. Fasten off.

OUTER EARS **D** (make 2)

Using size E-4 (3.5mm) hook and A, ch 13.

Foundation row (RS) 1 sc in 2nd ch from hook, 1 sc in each of rem ch, turn. *12 sc.*

Row 1 (patt row) Ch 1 (does NOT count as a st), 1 sc in each sc to end, turn.

Cont in sc throughout, work 2 rows more, ending with a WS row.

Next row (RS) Ch 1, work sc2tog over first 2 sc, 1 sc in each sc to last 2 sc, work sc2tog over last 2 sc, turn. *10 sc.*

Work even for 2 rows.

Next row (dec row) Ch 1, work sc2tog over first 2 sc, 1 sc in each sc to last 2 sc, work sc2tog over last 2 sc, turn.

Work even for 1 row.

Rep last 2 rows once more and then dec row again. *4 sc.* Fasten off.

INNER EARS **E** (make 2)

Using size E-4 (3.5mm) hook and B, ch 12.

Foundation row (RS) 1 sc in 2nd ch from hook, 1 sc in each of rem ch, turn. *11 sc.*

Row 1 (patt row) Ch 1 (does NOT count as a st), 1 sc in each sc to end, turn.

Cont in sc throughout, work 1 row more.

Next row (dec row) Ch 1, work sc2tog over first 2 sc, 1 sc in each sc to last 2 sc, work sc2tog over last 2 sc, turn.

Work even for 2 rows.

Rep dec row. *7 sc.*

Work even for 1 row.

Rep dec row. *5 sc.*

Next row Ch 1, work sc2tog over first 2 sc, 1 sc in next sc, work sc2tog over last 2 sc. *3 sc.*

Fasten off.

TAIL **F**

Using size E-4 (3.5mm) hook and B, ch 13.

Foundation round (RS) 1 sc in 2nd ch from hook, 1 sc in each of rem 11 ch, then working along other side of foundation ch, work 1 sc in each of next 12 ch, do not turn. *24 sc.*

Round 1 (RS) Ch 1, 1 sc in each of first 12 sc, ch 1, 1 sc in each of last 12 sc, join with a sl st to first sc.

Rep last round twice more.

Fasten off.

BLANKET **G**

Using size E-4 (3.5mm) hook and D, ch 20.

Foundation row (RS) 1 sc in 2nd ch from hook, 1 sc in next ch, *ch 1, skip 1 ch, 1 sc in next ch; rep from * to last ch, 1 sc in last ch, turn. *19 sts.*

Patt row 1 Ch 1 (does NOT count as a st), 1 sc in first sc, *ch 1, 1 sc in next 1-ch sp; rep from * to last 2 sc, ch 1, 1 sc in last sc, turn.

Patt row 2 Ch 1, 1 sc in first sc, *1 sc in next 1-ch sp, ch 1; rep from * to last 1-ch sp, 1 sc in last 1-ch sp, 1 sc in last sc, turn.

(Last 2 rows form patt when repeated.)

Work 43 rows more in patt, ending with a patt row 1. Fasten off.

Edging

With RS facing and using size E-4 (3.5mm) hook and C, work edging as follows:

Round 1 (RS) Join yarn with a sl st to first sc of previous row, ch 1, 1 sc in same place as sl st, then work in patt as set across row and cont working [ch 1, 1 sc] evenly down side-edge of blanket, along foundation row of blanket and up other side-edge, join with a sl st to first top of first sc. Fasten off.

STARS ⒣ (make 2)

Using size E-4 (3.5mm) hook and C, ch 2.

Round 1 (RS) 5 sc in 2nd ch from hook, join with a sl st to first sc.

(Do not turn at end of rounds, but work with RS always facing.)

Round 2 Ch 1, 2 sc same place as sl st, 2 sc in each of rem 4 sc, join with a sl st to first sc. *10 sc.*

Round 3 Ch 1, 1 sc in same place as sl st, ch 5, 1 sl st in 2nd ch from hook, 1 sc in next ch, 1 hdc in next ch, 1 dc in next ch, 1 dc in same place as first sc, skip next sc of previous round, *1 sc in next sc, ch 5, 1 sl st in 2nd ch from hook, 1 sc in next ch, 1 hdc in next ch, 1 dc in next ch, 1 dc in same place as first sc of this star point, skip next sc of previous round; rep from * 3 times more, join with a sl st to first sc. Fasten off.

TASSELS ⒤ (make 11)

Using C, wind yarn five times around a piece of cardboard 2in/5cm wide.

Thread a length of matching yarn onto a blunt-ended yarn needle and use this length of yarn to tie together strands of yarn at one end of cardboard; knot securely, leaving two long tail-ends of yarn at top of tassel.

Cut through strands at other end of cardboard. Wrap one tail-end several times around tassel, ½in/1.5cm from top, and secure. (Leave remaining tail-end at top, for sewing to blanket.) Trim tassel to 1½in/4cm long.

Make five more tassels using C, and five tassels using B—for a total of 11 tassels.

TO FINISH

Press pieces lightly on wrong side, following instructions on yarn label.

Body

With right sides together, join top seam of body pieces, leaving 2¾in/7cm open along back legs and ½in/1cm open along front of trunk.

Leaving 2¾in/7cm open along one back leg seam, sew underbody in place.

Turn right-side out, insert washable stuffing, and sew openings in seams closed.

Ears

With wrong sides together, sew inner ear pieces to outer ear pieces.

With inner ears facing forward, sew one side-edge of each ear to elephant so that foundation-chain edge faces outward.

Eyes

Using a blunt-ended yarn needle and B, work a large French knot for each eye as shown.

Tail

Fold tail in half lengthwise, and sew edges together. Sew tail to elephant as shown.

Sew one tassel in B to end of tail.

Blanket

Using a blunt-ended yarn needle and C, embroider four simple cross-stitches widthwise across center of blanket, each worked over two rows and one stitch apart.

Using B, embroider a large French knot at center of each cross-stitch.

Sew blanket to elephant, stitching along edges of blanket and for about 2in/5cm in each direction from center back seam.

Sew one star to blanket on each side of elephant by stitching a button to center of each star through both thicknesses.

ZIGZAG THROW

Bold, cheerful, warm, and cozy, the Zigzag Throw is perfect for brightening up any winter's day. Easily and quickly made in two pieces, this gorgeous throw needs to be taken out and shown off!

BEFORE YOU BEGIN

SIZE
The finished throw measures approximately 41¾in/106cm wide by 51½in/131cm long, including the edging.

YARN
Rowan *Pure Wool DK* (1¾oz/50g balls) as follows:

A	light turquoise (Pier 006)	11 balls
B	red (Kiss 036)	4 balls
C	mid green (Parsley 020)	3 balls
D	gold (Honey 033)	4 balls
E	orange (Tangerine 040)	2 balls

HOOK
Size E-4 (3.5mm) crochet hook

GAUGE
Approximately 22 sts and 9 rows to 4in/10cm measured over patt using size E-4 (3.5mm) crochet hook *or size necessary to obtain correct gauge.*

ABBREVIATIONS
dc2tog = [yo and insert hook in next st, yo and draw a loop through, yo and draw a loop through 2 loops on hook] twice, yo and draw through all 3 loops on hook—*one st decreased.* See also page 110.

GETTING STARTED

FIRST HALF OF THROW
The throw is made in two pieces joined together at the center.
Using size E-4 (3.5mm) hook and B, ch 225.
Foundation row (RS) 3 dc in 4th ch from hook,

*1 dc in each of next 5 ch, [dc2tog over next 2 ch] 3 times, 1 dc in each of next 5 ch, 4 dc in next ch; rep from * to end, turn.
Cut off B.
Change to A.
Row 1 (patt row) Ch 3, skip first 3 dc, 3 dc in next dc, *1 dc in each of next 5 dc, [dc2tog over next 2 dc] 3 times, 1 dc in each of next 5 dc, 4 dc in next dc; rep from *, working last 4 dc in 3rd of 3-ch, turn.
(Last row forms patt when repeated.)
Cont in patt throughout, work 6 rows more A, 1 row C, 1 row D, 1 row E, 1 row D, 1 row C, 7 rows A, 1 row C, 1 row D, 1 row E, 1 row D, 1 row C, 7 rows A, 1 row C, 1 row D, 1 row B, 1 row D, 1 row C, 5 rows A, 1 row B, 1 row A, 1 row B, 1 row A, 1 row B, 1 row E, 1 row D, 1 row C, 1 row A, 1 row B.
Next row (dec row) Using B, ch 3, skip first 3 dc, 2 dc in next dc, *1 dc in each of next 5 dc, [dc2tog over next 2 dc] 3 times, 1 dc in each of next 5 dc, 2 dc in next dc; rep from *, working last 2 dc in 3rd of 3-ch, turn.
Next row (dec row) Using B, ch 3, skip first 3 dc, *1 dc in each of next 4 dc, [dc2tog over next 2 dc] 3 times, 1 dc in each of next 5 dc; rep from *, working last dc in 3rd of 3-ch, turn.
Next row Using E, ch 3, skip first dc, 1 dc in each dc to end, 1 dc in 3rd of 3-ch, turn.
Next row Using D, ch 3, skip first dc, 1 dc in each dc to end, 1 dc in 3rd of 3-ch, turn.
Next row Using A, ch 3, skip first dc, 1 dc in each dc to end, 1 dc in 3rd of 3-ch, turn.
Fasten off.

SECOND HALF OF THROW
Work exactly as for first half.

TO FINISH
Sew two pieces together along straight edges of last rows.

Edging
With RS facing and using size E-4 (3.5mm) hook and B, work edging along one side-edge of

throw as follows:

Row 1 (RS) Join B with a sl st to beg of one side-edge, ch 3, then work a row of dc evenly along row-ends.

Fasten off.

Using B, work a row of dc in same way along other side-edge of throw but do not fasten off, instead cont

around edge of throw and work 1 sl st in next st (beg of foundation-chain edge), ch 3, then work a round of dc around edge, working decreases and increases to match those in patt along foundation-chain edges and 1 dc in each dc along side-edges, join with a sl st to 3rd of 3-ch at beg of round.

Press lightly on wrong side, following instructions on yarn label.

CROCHET HOW-TO TIPS

The projects in this book can be worked with a knowledge of only the most basic crochet stitches. None are too difficult for an average crocheter.

Here are some technical tips for beginners. Intermediate and experienced crocheters will find them useful as well if they haven't picked up their hooks for a while.

CHECKING YOUR CROCHET GAUGE

Be sure to check your gauge before beginning a project. Make a swatch about 6in/15cm square using the recommended yarn and hook size and working the stitch mentioned in Gauge section in the pattern. If your swatch has more stitches and rows to 4in/10cm than specified, try again using a larger hook size. If it has fewer stitches and rows to 4in/10cm, try again using a smaller hook size.

Obtaining the correct gauge is especially important when you are making a garment, so try your best to match the specified gauge before you start it. Gauge on small accessories or on motifs being used to make a large blanket or throw is not that important, so beginners are advised to try one of these as their very first project instead of a garment.

MAINTAINING AN EVEN GAUGE

Once you start crocheting your project, you may find that your gauge varies. Maintaining an even gauge in crochet is not as easy as it is with knitting, especially if the fabric is worked entirely in single crochet or half double crochet. Even very experienced crocheters sometimes have trouble keeping their single crochet gauge the same throughout an entire garment.

With practice your gauge will gradually even out. Try concentrating for a while on how tightly you are holding and releasing the yarn and on how tight or loose the loops feel on the hook as you make them. After concentrating for a several rows, the tension you have on the yarn and the tightness or looseness of the loops will start to become automatic.

If you leave a project for a few weeks and then go back to it, before working on it again, practice on a scrap swatch for about 20 to 30 minutes to get back into an even rhythm with your stitches.

COUNTING YOUR STITCHES

Crochet patterns give a "stitch count" at the end of some rows. This tells you how many stitches you should have after working that row. Counting your stitches from time to time is much more important with crochet than with knitting since it is easier to make a mistake in crochet.

Where a stitch count appears at the end of the foundation row or the first row after it, it is essential to count your stitches to make sure you have the right number. For single crochet, the turning chain (the chain stitch at the beginning of the row) is not counted as a stitch—only the actual single crochet stitches are counted. For taller stitches, however, the turning chains are counted as the first stitch of the row. This is usually explained clearly in the pattern.

Stitch counts are often given at the end of a row that has increases or decreases. It is not necessary to count your stitches every time a stitch count appears, but they are there in case you need them. Check at least occasionally when increasing and decreasing to make sure you have the right number of stitches.

Even when you are working your crochet even for many rows and the number of stitches is not changing, for example on a garment up to the armhole or on a scarf, it is worth counting your stitches occasionally. A lapse of concentration is not unusual and happens to all crocheters (no matter what their skill level), and this loss of concentration may cause you to inadvertently skip a stitch, especially at the edges of the crochet.

MARKING THE "RIGHT SIDE" OF THE CROCHET

Crochet pattern instructions always tell you which is the right side (abbreviated as "RS") of the fabric. To a beginner, this may seem unimportant when the crochet fabric itself is reversible, but it is often essential in the construction of the accessory or garment.

A good tip is to mark the right side of your crochet at the beginning when it is first mentioned. To do this, tie a short length of colored thread to the right side. Later in the pattern when the instructions tell you to hold the crochet with the right side facing you or to work a number of inches/centimeters and end with a wrong-side (WS) row, you will be glad the marker is there!

Don't cut off your "right-side" markers until the crochet is complete because you may need to refer to it when working an edging with the right or wrong side facing you or when sewing something together with the right or wrong sides facing each other.

WORKING CROCHET STRIPES

When changing to a new color for stripes, you can change at the beginning of the row that uses the new color, and this is usually what the instructions indicate.

However, a neater result is achieved if you change to the new color with the last "yarn over hook" of the previous row. If you do, the first chain in the new row will already be in the new color.

BLOCKING AND PRESSING CROCHET

Before you stitch together your crochet pieces, you should press them lightly if instructed to do so in the pattern instructions. This is your chance to smooth out handcrafted stitches and gently nudge your garment pieces into a more even shape.

Begin by pinning out each piece wrong-side up to the recommended measurements—this is called blocking. Check the pressing instructions on your yarn label to see if it is possible to press the yarn with a warm iron. If pressing is not recommended, then lay a clean damp cloth over the crochet and leave the cloth and crochet until both are completely dry.

If you can use a warm iron on your yarn, then lay a clean damp cloth over it and gently press the crochet over the damp cloth to create steam. Do not drag or slide the iron over the cloth, but lift it up to move it. Do not press down on the iron when it is in place or leave it too long in one place or you will squash the natural texture of the crochet.

Remove the cloth and leave the crochet until it is completely dry.

SEAMS ON CROCHET

Take your time when finishing your crochet. Don't rush—and don't hesitate to undo seams (or edgings) and start again if they don't look right the first time. It may feel frustrating at the time, but it is worth the extra effort and patience.

Both overcast stitches and backstitch are good for sewing seams on crochet pieces. Using a blunt-ended yarn needle, test which seam you like best for your accessory or garment by trying it out on two small swatches.

Some crocheters like to work seams with crochet stitches. To do this, hold the pieces with the right sides together and work a line of chain stitches through both layers very close to the edge. Although this is a quick way to join pieces together, it may create a bulkier seam than you want for a child's garment, so be sure to test it before trying it on the garment pieces.

For seams on toys, I find that the best seam to use, where possible, is backstitch—for example, when stitching together the toy's main body pieces. Simply place the right sides together, sew the seam close to the edge with small, even backstitches, then turn right side out.

Perservere and you will find the type of seam that works best for you.

CROCHET ABBREVIATIONS

The following are the abbreviations used in the patterns in this book. Special abbreviations are given with individual patterns.

alt	alternate
beg	begin(ning)
ch	chain
ch sp	chain space
cm	centimeter(s)
cont	continu(e)(ing)
dc	double crochet
dec	decreas(e)(ing)
DK	double knitting (a lightweight yarn)
foll	follow(s)(ing)
g	gram(s)
hdc	half double crochet
in	inch(es)
inc	increas(e)(ing)
m	meter(s)
mm	millimeter(s)
oz	ounce(s)
patt	pattern
rem	remain(s)(ing)
rep	repeat(s)(ing)
RS	right side
sc	single crochet
sl st	slip stitch
sp	space
st(s)	stitch(es)
tog	together
WS	wrong side
yd	yard(s)
yo	yarn over hook

* = Repeat instructions after asterisk or between asterisks as many times as instructed.

[ ] = Repeat instructions inside brackets as many times as instructed; or work all instructions inside brackets into same place.

CROCHET TERMINOLOGY

English language crochet terminology is not the same in all countries. This book was written with the crochet terminology used in the US. If you have learned crochet using the United Kingdom terminology, use this list to find the meaning of the US terms and their abbreviations:

US	UK
slip stitch (sl st)	slip stitch (ss)
single crochet (sc)	double crochet (dc)
half double crochet (hdc)	half treble crochet (htr)
double crochet (dc)	treble crochet (tr)
treble crochet (tr)	double treble (dtr)
double treble (dtr)	triple treble (trtr)
triple treble (trtr)	quadruple treble (qtr)
skip	miss
yarn over hook (yo)	yarn round hook (yrh)

YARN INFORMATION

For the best results, use the Rowan yarns recommended in the patterns. If, however, you are attempting to use a substitute yarn, be sure to use a yarn that matches the original in type, and buy according to length of yarn per ball, rather than by the weight of the ball. The specifications of the yarns used in this book are given below. The recommended gauge for stockinette stitch is provided for each yarn because this gives an accurate guide to the thickness of the yarn when your are trying to find a substitute.

Shade numbers are given in each crochet pattern, but these are only suggestions. There can be no guarantee that every color will still be available by the time you use this book, as shades change frequently with fashion trends.

ROWAN COTTON GLACE

A fine-weight cotton yarn; 100 percent cotton; approximately 126yd/115m per 1¾oz/50g ball; recommended gauge—23 sts and 32 rows to 4in/10cm measured over stockinette stitch using size 3–5 (3.25–3.75mm) knitting needles.

ROWAN 4-PLY COTTON

A super-fine-weight cotton yarn; 100 percent cotton; approximately 186yd/170m per 1¾oz/50g ball; recommended gauge—27–29 sts and 37–39 rows to 4in/10cm measured over stockinette stitch using size 2–3 (3–3.25mm) knitting needles.

ROWAN 4-PLY SOFT

A super-fine-weight wool yarn; 100 percent merino wool; approximately 191yd/175m per 1¾oz/50g ball; recommended gauge—28 sts and 36 rows to 4in/10cm measured over stockinette stitch using size 3 (3.25mm) knitting needles.

ROWAN PURE WOOL DK

A double-knitting-weight yarn; 100 percent super-wash wool yarn; approximately 137yd/125m per 1¾oz/50g ball; recommended gauge—22 sts and 30 rows to 4in/10cm measured over stockinette stitch using size 6 (4mm) knitting needles.

STANDARD YARN WEIGHT SYSTEM

Categories of yarn, gauge ranges, and recommeded hook sizes from the Craft Yarn Council of America.
YarnStandards.com

Yarn Weight Symbol and Category Names	1 SUPER FINE	2 FINE	3 LIGHT	4 MEDIUM	5 BULKY	6 SUPER BULKY
Type of Yarns in Category	Sock, Fingering, Baby	Sport, Baby	DK, Light Worsted	Worsted, Afghan, Aran	Chunky, Craft, Rug	Bulky, Roving
Crochet Gauge* Ranges in Single Crochet to 4in/10cm	21–32 sts	16–20 sts	12–17 sts	11–14 sts	8–11 sts	5–9 sts
Recommended Hook in Metric Size Range	2.25–3.5mm	3.5–4.5mm	4.5–5.5mm	5.5–6.5mm	6.5–9mm	9mm and larger
Recommended Hook in U.S. Size Range	B-1 to E-4	E-4 to 7	7 to I-9	I-9 to K-10½	K-10½ to M-13	M-13 and larger

* GUIDELINES ONLY: The above reflect the most commonly used gauges and hook sizes for specific yarn categories.

YARN ADDRESSES

Contact the distributors listed here to find a supplier of Rowan handknitting yarns near you. For countries not listed, contact the main office in the UK or the Rowan website: www.knitrowan.com

USA: Westminster Fibers Inc., 165 Ledge Street, Nashua, NH 03060. Tel: 1-800-445-9276. E-mail: rowan@westminsterfibers.com www.westminsterfibers.com

AUSTRALIA: Australian Country Spinners, 314 Albert Street, Brunswick, Victoria 3056. Tel: (03) 9380 3888.

AUSTRIA: Coats Harlander GmbH, Autokaderstrasse 31, A-1230 Wien. Tel: (01) 27716-0. Fax: (01) 27716-228.

BELGIUM: Coats Benelux, Ring Oost 14A, Ninove, 9400. Tel: 054 318989. E-mail: sales.coatsninove@coats.com

CANADA: Same as USA.

CHINA: Coats Shanghai Ltd., No. 9 Building, Doasheng Road, Songjiang Industrial Zone, Shanghai. Tel: 86 21 5774 3733 Ext 329. Fax: 86 21 5774 3768. E-mail: victor.li@coats.com

DENMARK: Coats HP A/S, Nannagade 28, 2200 Copenhagen. Tel: 35 86 90 50. Fax: 35 82 15 10.

FINLAND: Coats Opti Oy, Ketjutie 3, 04220 Kerava. Tel: (358) 9 274871. Fax: (358) 9 2748 7330. E-mail: coatsopti.sales@coats.com www.coatscrafts.com

FRANCE: Coats Steine, 100 avenue du Général de Gaulle, 18 500 Mehun-Sur-Yèvre. Tel: 02 48 23 12 30. Fax: 02 48 23 12 40. www.coatscrafts.fr

GERMANY: Coats GMbH, Kaiserstrasse 1, D-79341 Kenzingen. Tel: 07162-14346. www.coatsgmbh.de

HOLLAND: Coats Benelux, Ring Oost 14A, Ninove, 9400. Tel: 0346 35 37 00. E-mail: sales.coatsninove@coats.com

HONG KONG: Coats China Holding Ltd., 19/F., Millenium City 2, 378 Kwun Tong Road, Kwun Tong, Kowloon. Tel: (852) 2798 6886. Fax: (852) 2305 0311. Email: jackie.li@coats.com

ICELAND: Rowan at Storkurinn, Laugavegi 59, ICE-101. Tel: 551 8258.

ITALY: dl srl, Via Piave, 24-26, 20016 Pero, Milan. Tel: 02 339 101 80.

JAPAN: Puppy-Jardin Co. Ltd., 3-8 11 Kudanminami, Chiyodaku, Hiei Kudan Bldg. 5F, Tokyo. Tel: 3222-7076. Fax: 3222-7066. E-mail: info@rowan-jaeger.com

KOREA: Coats Korea Co. Ltd., 5F Kuckdong B/D, 935-40 Bangbae-Dong, Seocho-Gu, Seoul. Tel: 82-2-521-6262. Fax: 82-2-521-5181.

MEXICO: Estambres Crochet SA de CV, Aaron Saenz 1891-7, Monterrey, NL 64650. Tel: +52 (81) 8335-3870.

NEW ZEALAND: ACS New Zealand, 1 March Place, Belfast, Christchurch. Tel: 64-3-323-6665. Fax: 64-3-323-6660.

NORWAY: Coats Knappehuset AS, Pb 100 Ulset, 5873 Bergen. Tel: (47) 55 53 93 00. Fax: (47) 55 53 93 93.

SINGAPORE: Golden Dragon Store, 101 Upper Cross Street #02-51, People's Park Centre, Singapore 058357. Tel: (65) 65358454. E-mail: gdscraft@hotmail.com

SOUTH AFRICA: Arthur Bales Ltd., 62 4th Avenue, Linden, Johannesburg 2195. Tel: (27) 118 882 401. Fax: (27) 117 826 137. E-mail: arthurb@new.co.za

SPAIN: Oyambre, Pau Claris 145, 80009 Barcelona. Tel/Fax: (34) 93 4872672.

SWEDEN: Coats Expotex AB, Division Craft, Box 297, 401 24 Göteborg. Tel: (46) 33 720 79 00. Fax: (46) 31 47 16 50.

SWITZERLAND: Coats Stoppel AG, CH-5300 Tungi (AG). Tel: 056 298 12 20. Fax: 056 298 12 50.

TAIWAN: Laiter Wool Knitting Co. Ltd., 10-1 313 Lane, Sec 3, Chung Ching North Road, Taipei. Tel: (886) 2 2596 0269. Fax: (886) 2 2598 0619.

THAILAND: Global Wide Trading, 10 Lad Prao Soi 88, Bangkok 10310. Tel: 00 662 933 9019. Fax: 00 662 933 9110.

UK: Rowan, Green Lane Mill, Holmfirth, West Yorkshire HD9 2DX, England. Tel: +44 (0) 1484 681881. Fax: +44 (0) 1484 687920. E-mail: mail@knitrowan.com www.knitrowan.com

ACKNOWLEDGMENTS

Many thanks to all who were involved with this book and for all your hard work!
Especially Susan for wise words, wisdom and guidance, Sally and Penny for expertise and patience, and François for his abounding talent and for making everything look lovely!

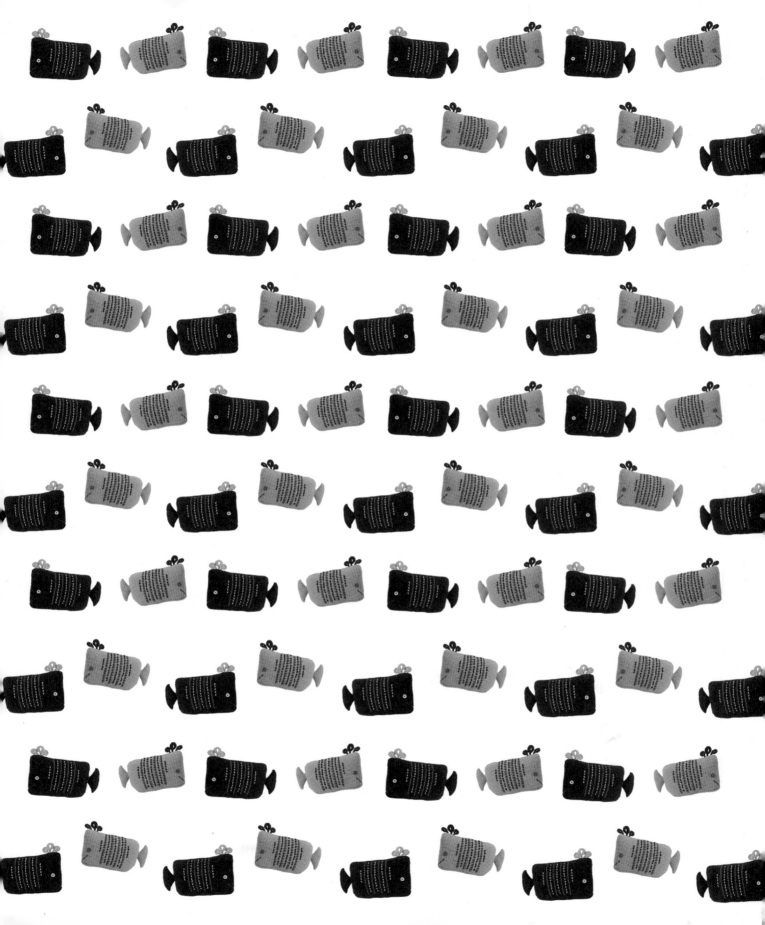